HIDDEN
HISTORY
of
MONMOUTH
COUNTY

HIDDEN
HISTORY
of
MONMOUTH
COUNTY

Rick Geffken and Muriel J. Smith

Forewords by Allan Dean &
Christina Johnson

THE
History
PRESS

Published by The History Press
Charleston, SC
www.historypress.net

Front cover: *The Highlands of the Neversink and the Twin Lights* by an unknown artist, after 1872. *McKay Imaging Photography*.

Back cover: *Sea Bright Beach* by Michel Jacobs, circa 1940. *Monmouth County Historical Association*; *inset*: *Main Lighthouse, Sandy Hook: Southwest View* by Franklin Patterson, 1879. *McKay Imaging Photography*.

First published 2019

Manufactured in the United States

ISBN 9781467142038

Library of Congress Control Number: 2019939733

Notice: The information in this book is true and complete to the best of our knowledge. It is offered without guarantee on the part of the author or The History Press. The author and The History Press disclaim all liability in connection with the use of this book.

DEDICATION

This book is dedicated to future Monmouth County generations in the hope that they will learn and profit from everyone who has ever lived in, worked in, visited or experienced the best New Jersey has to offer.

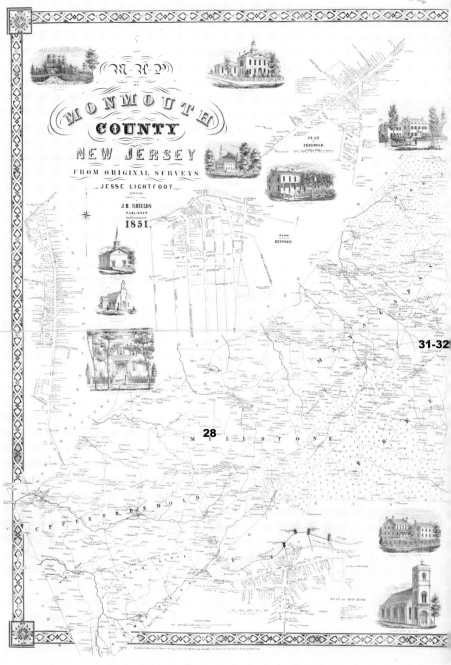

The numbers on this 1851 Jesse Lightfoot map of Monmouth County correspond to the settings/locations discussed in those chapters in this book. *Monmouth County Archives.*

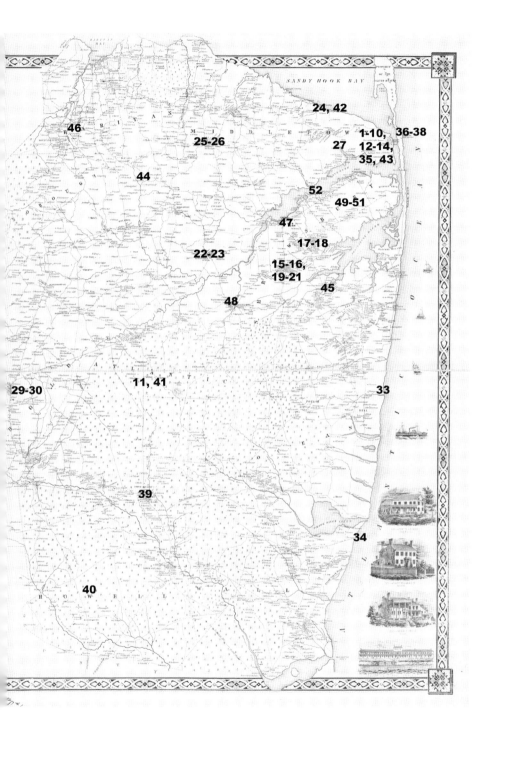

CONTENTS

CONTENTS

FOREWORDS

Whether it is the uproarious Highlands rum-running days and a cop on the beat or a casual walk through History House at Sandy Hook's Fort Hancock, Muriel J. Smith shares with the reader a warm and cozy story of bygone days. Her column in the *Herald* has enlightened many readers new to the region and caused more than one salty native to delight in a new discovery at home.

Muriel has put decades of local knowledge to work as she informs people, through her writings, about their own roots in and around Monmouth County, New Jersey. She has a long personal history with government, political and business leaders in the area, which has served her well over her more than sixty years working in local journalism.

Her column, "History and Happenings," appears in the *Atlantic Highlands Herald* (ahherald.com), and each week, Muriel delves into local histories or a travelogue of her adventures in the United States and around the world. I feel confident this new book will let others know what readers of the *Herald* have known all along, and I congratulate Muriel and her coauthor, Rick Geffken, for treating others to the depth of their knowledge and charm of their stories. Congratulations on another job well done.

—Allan Dean, publisher/editor, *Atlantic Highlands Herald*
Atlantic Highlands, New Jersey

Rick Geffken has been delighting readers of the weekly *Two River Times* for several years with glimpses of how life was lived in our Monmouth County, New Jersey towns. With his keen eye for detail and reporter's ear for a surprising revelation, Rick's interesting stories and portraits often land on page one.

Over the years, his travels to our thirteen towns have enabled him to tell stories about a forgotten submarine inventor who toiled in Atlantic Highlands, the first Jersey Shore–resort tycoon on Sandy Hook and Shrewsbury Borough's tiny museum. He has interviewed war veterans, historic home renovators, maritime historians, a colonial garment seamstress, graveyard restoration specialists and Civil War reenactors.

Rick's humble personality, kind manner and intelligence have allowed him to gain the trust of local history caretakers. In a society both intrigued and fatigued by the tantalizing tidbits streaming on our social-media feeds, his articles reassure readers that quality work, acts of service, works of beauty and leaps of imagination can endure and inspire.

—Christina Johnson, news editor, the *Two River Times*
Red Bank, New Jersey

Acknowledgements

A writer is only as good as her sources, so my first, most prolific thanks go to the Molly Pitchers, Bill McCoys, clammers, builders, military heroes and those like them who gave me the heartbeat of my stories. I thank also my grown children and their spouses—my oldest daughter, Kathy, and Bobby (even though Kathy died in 2008, he's still my Bobby!); Michelle; Jimbo and Stacy; and Tracie and Chris—for giving me the time and enthusiasm to live the history and teach them about the stories and people about whom I write. I especially thank Jim and Tracie for sticking with me and keeping me composed through this first book I am coauthoring with another writer. I thank my coauthor, Rick, as well, for learning to accept my style, my lack of concern for organization and my neophyte knowledge of computer technology.

I thank the historians who have always helped me: Freeholder Lillian Burry, Shrewsbury mayor Donald Burden, Freehold historian Kevin Coyne, Freehold mayor Nolan Higgins, Twin Lights Friends chairman Mark Stewart, Doug Paviluk (of the *Monmouth Journal*) and Allan Dean (of the *Atlantic Highlands Herald*). Also, thanks to my many dear friends from Highlands, Atlantic Highlands and Freehold who buoy my spirits with their overabundant praise for my writing, two generations of the Swartz family, Doctor Harry and Renee and Dr. Steve and you, the reader, for having an interest in preserving Monmouth County history for future generations.

—Muriel Smith

My sincere thanks to Christina Johnson, my editor at *The Two River Times*, whose direction and patience helps me become a better journalist; and to the paper's publisher, Dominic DiPiero, for providing me the forum for my articles on Monmouth County people and history.

My friend and coauthor of my first book, Don Burden, is a constant supporter who always has positive suggestions for story ideas. Christ Church Shrewsbury's historian, Bob Kelly, is a great resource and another friend. I'm indebted to Randy Gabrielan, upon whom I can always count for insight into any and all historical references about Monmouth County.

Others who have helped include Frank Barricelli, Robin Blair, Amanda Mae Edwards, John Fabiano, Susie Sandlass Gardiner, Claire Garland, Pati Githens, Joe Grabas, Walt Guenther, Joe Hammond, Scott Longfield, Elsalyn Palmisano, Gary Saretzky, Bob Schoeffling, George Severini, Leigh Shaffer, Rob Shomo, Stacey Slowinski, Rich Veit, Keith Wells and Melissa Ziobro. I hope the people profiled in my articles get the credit they deserve for their generous contributions to our shared history.

And, I particularly want to thank my friend and coauthor, Muriel Smith, who made this project almost as much fun as an Irish wake.

—Rick Geffken

INTRODUCTION

For two longtime residents of Monmouth County, it was love at first sight regarding everything about Monmouth County—the hills, the ocean, the rivers, the people…but most of all, the history. Rick Geffken summered at the shore in his youth and moved to Middletown permanently just after high school; Muriel Smith arrived as an eighteen-year-old bride and raised her family in Highlands.

It seems inevitable, therefore, that these two writers and historians would connect, compare their stories and realize that they could offer readers different approaches to subjects great and small about the county they've called home for so long.

Rick, a former teacher (as if that adjectival descriptive were possible), loves precise wording—a nod, no doubt, to his Jesuit schooling. Muriel notes that he is prolific with his descriptions of people and places. Muriel, an ever-inquisitive journalist (obviously redundant), revels in capturing her audience in her first paragraphs, then carrying her readers through to the last words with bits of mystery and intrigue. Rick is astonished at how quickly she can write a story and make a deadline.

This compilation of their articles features stories Muriel and Rick tell with a vivacity that comes not only from loving their subjects but from their joy in sharing these tales with others.

The book is meant to be read easily and often, whether one takes in a single story at a time or sets aside a few hours to pore through them all. It's meant to be picked up to settle an argument, relive a particular memory or learn how it all began. And, in the end, the authors hope their affection for this very special part of New Jersey is shared by everyone.

Part I: The Bayshore

I

A Piece of History on a Busy Highlands–Sea Bright Bridge

By Muriel J. Smith

The change to the name of the bridge that spans the Shrewsbury River between Highlands and Sea Bright was finalized in 2011, when the state general assembly approved Senate Bill 2073. The bill had already passed the state senate, offering a change of name to honor late Highlands native, Middletown businessman, state assemblyman and senator and U.S. Naval Reserve captain Joseph A. Azzolina.

Those who were old friends from even before they worked together at the Senate level took the lead in the action to honor Captain Azzolina. Senator Sean Kean knew Azzolina from his reputation as an assemblyman beginning in 1966, then later worked with him in the assembly when Kean was elected to his first term in 2002. Senator Joe Kyrillos, who retired in 2018 and was himself honored when the Red Bank Bridge was named for him, knew Azzolina when the latter owned the *Courier* weekly newspaper in Kyrillos's hometown and the young then-assemblyman dropped off his own press releases for publication.

Azzolina lived in Middletown with his family and was a successful businessman, growing his family's first business on Miller Street to the Food Basket supermarket on the main street in Highlands, then to the Food Circus in Middletown and eventually to the heart of the Foodtown Enterprises still in the family today. He knew the Kyrillos family well. Joe Kyrillos always commented on how his friend Joe loved New Jersey, especially Monmouth County, and how the businessman's immigrant parents had started their own small market, the one on Miller Street in Highlands, shortly after arriving from their native Italy.

Senator Jennifer Beck had worked side by side with Azzolina when he was an assemblyman and she was his chief of staff. But Beck had worked with and known Azzolina even earlier and always referred to him as her mentor. She spoke of his special affinity for the Bayshore and, at the time of introducing the bill to name the bridge, said how honored and humbled the sailor would have been about the honor given to his memory.

The new construction was designed to eliminate the bridge openings that backed up traffic along the state highway. The construction on the higher bridge included high railings, putting an end to the summer ritual of daring Highlands kids who reveled at jumping from its highest peaks to the channel below—a ritual a young Azzolina also pursued. Yet, even the new higher bridge could not quite put an end to traffic tie-ups on sunny days when everyone wants to go to the Gateway National Recreation Area at Sandy Hook.

Trying to put a Sunday early-afternoon ride along Ocean Avenue in Sea Bright into a book like *Hidden History of Monmouth County* is only possible because of a recent forty-five-minute trip from the Sea Bright side of the Highlands to the Rumson bridges. There was plenty of time to reminisce about the 1950s—a time when the same trip at the same time on a sunshine-y weekend day would have taken three minutes (maybe five minutes if one keeps below the speed limits).

The new and beautiful Captain Joseph Azzolina Memorial Bridge is successful in its purpose of keeping boat traffic sailing smoothly along the Shrewsbury River. No longer do bridgetenders stroll out, close the gates and stop traffic only to reappear again at the same slow pace to reverse the pattern and let vehicular traffic pass once the boats are safely through. There was even a time when the bridge opened due to the demand of river traffic; this was somewhat improved when the bridge openings were changed to twice an hour, so even boats had to occasionally wait—or improve the timing of their arrival—at the bridge.

The old Highlands–Sea Bright Bridge opened to allow marine traffic to pass, but for the vehicular traffic on the state highway between the two communities, the new, improved situation only works if drivers are courteous, polite and intelligent. On a recent weekend, this was a tough combination to find.

A journey toward Rumson from Middletown along Route 36 at 1:00 p.m. on a July Sunday seemed like it would be a quick trip. However, once the vehicle rounded the last curve before Our Lady of Perpetual Help Church, it was evident the Oceanic Bridge in Locust would have been the longer—in terms of distance—but better option.

Traffic in the "through" lane (the one not heading into Sandy Hook) was moving slowly but steadily, but one wonders why the lane heading into Sandy Hook was stopped. West of the bridge, two signs had been posted indicating that the park was closed. There was plenty of opportunity for drivers to choose other options rather than continue across the bridge—options that included going under the bridge, into the wonderful town of Highlands, and visiting a river beach that offered the same water, same beautiful sand, but simply a lot quieter and much calmer—far better than sitting in a car with impatient kids, angry drivers and no beach in sight for an afternoon's enjoyment. Another pleasant option could be going down into Buttermilk Valley and perhaps stopping at Hartshorne Park for a walk through the woods or heading back to Atlantic Highlands for a stroll through the yacht harbor, or heading up the hill to either the magnificent Twin Lights or via Portland Road to see the newly renovated defense site complete with that huge gun from the Battleship *New Jersey* (and where the temperature inside the battery hovers somewhere in the 70s!).

Yet, the cars were at a stop at the top of the bridge, all waiting to get into Sandy Hook…for what? To turn around and head back? Didn't drivers see signs saying the park was closed? To visit the Sandy Hook Lighthouse? Getting to Twin Lights would take less time, offer more spectacular views and include a sensational museum full of great history and artifacts. Does anyone even know a Congressional Medal of Honor recipient from the Spanish-American War was once a lighthouse keeper here?

It was around the middle of the bridge where the rudeness began to show. Among all those cars not going to Sandy Hook were a half-dozen drivers who were going to Sandy Hook but knew they could move faster in the opposite lane and cut in at the last minute. Forget about the anger that caused, the stopping it created in both lanes, the near-misses and the language children shouldn't be hearing. Think of the idiocy of it. Why would you still try so hard to cut into a lane heading to where the park folks were going to turn you back anyway? Even the smarter folks who made that apparently illegal turn at the end of the bridge to head back toward Highlands didn't impede traffic as much.

But something happened to drivers on the other side of the bridge once the vehicles going to Sandy Hook were out of the way. Suddenly, they seemed nicer, calmer, politer. The cars coming off the Hook, turned back by rangers who advised them once again that the signs were telling the truth and the park really was closed to beachgoers, had to get into that lane of traffic heading through Sea Bright. But they were waiting in line for a break, waiting patiently in line for a break—and they got it. Drivers continuing to Sea Bright from Highlands began to cooperate with the outgoing Hook cars; they were taking turns, the way it should be done! One car would continue on the road, and the next car would pause to enable a car leaving the Hook to blend in, then another road car would proceed, then a Hook car would blend in, alternating one car at a time. There were hand waves, signs of thanks, even smiles. It worked! Alternating cars actually worked! No more foul language or angry looks—instead, there were smiles and signs of appreciation. Life was getting better.

Because of the added traffic, the situation slowly continued along Ocean Avenue, steadily moving with no horn-blowing, no fist shakes—nothing but peaceful driving. What's more, drivers were not only stopping at cross streets to let other cars out, they were even stopping to allow those leaving the "rocks" to cross safely. More waves, more thanks, more smiles.

For the drivers, there was time to enjoy the unique houses along the Strip. Sadly, these are not the gracious old Victorian mansions that provided many a drill for the volunteers in the Highlands, Sea Bright, Rumson, Atlantic Highlands and Navesink fire companies in the 1950s and 1960s, when alarms sounded in the middle of the night and these volunteers rushed out to "save the fireplace" and surrounding homes. But they are magnificent new dwellings, both single and multifamily, that are well-kept, attractive and a credit to Sea Bright.

The twice-hourly bridge closure at the Rumson bridge slowed traffic somewhat, but people didn't seem to mind so much. At that point, there were walkers to watch, cyclists to see and motorcyclists who carefully wended their way through it all, creating their own lanes but safely moving forward. When there was some type of emergency in the north end of Sea Bright that required police to travel from the center of town, cars moved quickly and safely to the sides of the road to create a lane for the police cars to pass.

Ocean Avenue is the same width it was sixty years ago. The ocean is still the same, although it is not visible because of the higher seawall. The landside view is different, and the river is still vibrant to see in many areas. Driving slowly along the Strip can truly be an enjoyable experience once angry and frustrated drivers realize it doesn't get them there any faster, happier or more safely than simply accepting how popular we've become and enjoying the ride.

—From the *Atlantic Highlands Herald,* July 30, 2018

A Historic Army Site, a Historic Navy Gun Barrel

By Muriel J. Smith

A piece of the Battleship *New Jersey*, BB62, is an intricate vision and a striking spectacle as part of the Monmouth County Park System's Hartshorne Woods in Highlands and Middletown.

The weapon is part of Battery Lewis, one of the two batteries built at the former army site at the top of the Highlands hill during World War II as the main defense for New York Harbor. The site, known as Rocky Point, is part of an educational exhibit highlighting the area's involvement and importance in World War II.

Battery Lewis is a six-hundred-foot-long casemated battery with two sixteen-inch-caliber gun emplacements connected by a corridor housing ammunition storage and powder rooms. It is the only sixteen-inch-caliber gun battery in the state and is constructed of steel and thick reinforced concrete covered by earth.

The battery was designed to withstand battleship and aerial attacks and had two sixteen-inch-caliber navy MK11 M1 guns on army carriages mounted in it in May 1943. The guns placed in Battery Lewis were originally designed to be mounted on navy battleships and are able to fire armor-piercing projectiles that are sixteen inches in diameter and weigh more than two tons, with a range stretching from Point Pleasant Beach to Long Beach, New York.

In 2016, the Monmouth County Park System began extensive planning for repairs and improvements to prepare Battery Lewis for interpretation and public visitation. The first phase of work, restoring the concrete on the two casemate canopies and wing walls, was funded by the Monmouth County Friends of the Parks; the site itself, originally known as the Navesink Military Reservation, was nominated to be added to the National Register of Historic Places and designed so that visitors can walk from one end of the battery to the other, explore the rooms within it and learn through exhibits and guided tours about the coastal defenses of the United States.

The final phase of the Battery Lewis restoration included interior repairs, utility and drainage improvements and the display of the gun barrel. In addition to the rooms off the corridor and the gun barrel, exhibits focus on the military past of the area as well as the unique geography and landscape of Highlands, the Hartshorne legacy and the creation of Hartshorne Woods Park. Exhibits also include an overhead trolley showing the steel ammunition service, artifacts (including sixteen-inch projectiles donated by the Battleship *New Jersey* Museum in Camden), historical photographs and reminiscences of veterans who served at the site.

The Monmouth County Board of Recreation Commissioners authorized application to the Navy Inactive Ships Program at Norfolk, Virginia, to acquire one of the barrels from the Battleship *New Jersey*, BB62, to replace the original gun that was there in the 1940s and subsequently dismantled and removed. The navy approved that application and arranged for the transport of the barrel to the county park. Now in place in the battery, the gun helps tell the story of the area's military past and Battery Lewis along with an overview of the park's history and landscape.

The former army site, which was later used an air force base during the Korean conflict, was part of the Hartshorne estate and was purchased by the government in 1942 because of its elevation and location at the southern entrance to New York Harbor. Over the next two years, the army reservation was built as part of Harbor Defense headquartered at Sandy Hook for the purpose of denying enemy ships access to New York Bay. After World War II, the guns were removed at all coastal batteries (including Battery Lewis), cut up on-site and sold as scrap metal. Troop housing and a one-hundred-foot observation tower were also demolished by the army before the property became the Highlands Air Force Station (later the Highlands Army Air Defense Site) from 1949 to 1974.

When the 224-acre property was declared surplus, the government authorized two no-cost transfers to Monmouth County in 1974 and 1984. The entire Hartshorne Woods County Park, which stretches from Highlands to Middletown along Navesink Avenue, is 787 acres in size and receives more than a quarter of a million visitors a year.

The transfer of BB62's gun caused flurries of excitement for many days and drew large crowds during the gun's journey from storage in Norfolk, Virginia, to its new home at Rocky Point. The trip included not only trains and trucks but three cranes (one in Virginia and two in New Jersey), a flurry of permits authorizing the travel along the way, road surveys, police escorts and numerous other details; it was completed at a cost of $180,000, culminating a project that had begun four years earlier.

The original sixteen-inch-caliber navy Mark seven-gun barrel began its journey by train from Virginia to South Amboy, then was transferred to another train for an arrival in Red Bank, where it was placed in the Conrail rail yard on Central Avenue until arrangements could be completed for the next leg of its journey. The sixty-five-foot-long gun barrel was then transported by tractor-trailer along Route 35 to New Monmouth Road, then over to Route 36 for access to Hartshorne Woods Park via Portland Road.

Ironically, when the gun barrel from the Battleship *New Jersey* made its final turn off the state highway before advancing up the hill to its new home at Hartshorne Woods Park, it passed within feet of the Captain Joseph Azzolina Bridge (formerly the Highlands–Sea Bright Bridge). The bridge was named for Highlands native and former naval officer, state senator and assemblyman Joseph Azzolina, who served aboard the USS *New Jersey* and was instrumental in bringing the ship back to the Garden State to serve as a museum. The ship is the most decorated battleship for combat actions in United States history and served in every war from World War II until it was decommissioned in 1991 after twenty-one years of active service, a Navy Unit Commendation and nineteen battle and campaign stars.

—From the *Atlantic Highlands Journal*, June 24, 2018

ATLANTIC HIGHLANDS IN THE GOOD OLD DAYS

By Muriel J. Smith

Any of the old-timers in and around Atlantic Highlands will tell you of the "good old days"—the amusement park at the river beach, the milkman who delivered milk to your door, the schools and churches that were an integral part of everyone's life. But among the collection of things from the past that still keep Helen Marchetti so proud and happy she's a native of the borough is a treasured little gray book that was offered to newcomers be they settlers or vacationers. The booklet, *Atlantic Highlands New Jersey*, features close to two hundred businesses and businesspeople, if you include all the notary publics, nurses and well-diggers who made their livings here.

It was 1931, the start of the era just after the Roaring Twenties, and John R. Snedecker was in the second year of his second term as mayor (he would go on to win a third term in November), and the little booklet bragged that the tax rate here "is one of the lowest in Monmouth County and compares favorably with any municipality in the State."

Most of the descriptions included within the book could be repeated now: "the joy of a country home coupled with city conveniences…the joy of a garden," and so on, but with the added promise, "we can guarantee the fertile soil if you will make your own garden." The area offered, according to the booklet, "Class A" weather, but then, the brochure proclaimed, "how could it be otherwise in a town so ideally located…hills and valleys touching hands, providing scenes of the Atlantic Ocean…from our Ocean Blvd on clear days, one may easily distinguish the sky-scrapers of Manhattan and also obtain a splendid view of Fort Hancock…one of our Coast Defenses."

But it's the classified directory in the booklet that especially recalls famous local names, former and current businesses and a genuinely great community. Five different amusements are included: the amusement park on Avenue A (the phone number was 497), the Atlantic Theater on First Avenue, the Billiard Parlor at First and Highland Avenues, the indoor golf course on First Avenue and the tennis club on Bayview.

There was only one architect in town, L. Jerome Aimar, whose office was at the corner of Memorial Drive and East Avenue, and one engineer, H.O. Todd, with his office on Memorial Drive. However, there were seven builders and contractors, including Carhart Construction, D.A. Caruso, John Grary, B.G. Martin, W.B. Mount, J.E. Stone and C.A Wright. There were four painting contractors and two electricians. There was even a sawmill operated by William Irwin on West Garfield Avenue.

There were four doctors (physicians Fred Bullwinkel, A. Rosenthal, John VanMater and Walter White) and one dentist, Thomas McVey, whose dental office was at 95 First Avenue. There were eleven women listed as either registered or practical nurses, including some names that are still familiar today, like Edna Dender, Mable Mount, Florence or Dorothy Gaffey and Lottie Loux. Antonides's and Shannon's were drugstores practically across the street from each other on First Avenue, and Bridle and Latham in Navesink and Romeo Brothers on First Avenue were the two local florists.

Mack Davis, Tom Kelly and George Keyes provided all the ice needed for the four hotels (and so many others) in town, and the Red Bank Steam Dye Works at 77 First Avenue took care of all the dyeing and cleaning business.

There were four separate law offices before some of the attorneys later merged, like John Pillsbury with Snyder and Roberts, all in the same building at 97 First Avenue, with John Sweeney a few doors down and Edgar Cook practicing on Asbury Avenue.

There was no shortage of places to buy quality meats, groceries, candy or ice cream. At least four stores had ice cream parlors, including Stryker's Market at First and Center Avenues, and Wagner's, also on First Avenue; Jagger's and Blom's markets, both also on First Avenue, prided themselves on the quality of their meat, fish and provisions. Some of the other general markets included American Stores, James Butler, Brookes & Company, W.V. Crawford, Economy Stores, William Nachamks, West End and White's Groceries. It was easy to shop close to home and find competitive prices.

It was interesting to see that thirteen residents, some of them attorneys or bankers, some businessmen in other fields, were listed as notary publics, and another six were plumbers, with one—Walter Williams on Bay View Avenue—also noting that he was a tinsmith.

There was only one milliner in town: Bertha A. Briggs, who sold the fashionable headwear at her shop at 96 First Avenue. The one newspaper, the *Atlantic Highlands Journal*, was also the only printer in town, and one window-cleaner, Arnold Varrar, was the only person listed in that particular business. The A.M. and Sons Posten's Funeral Home was at 25 First Avenue at this time, and Jake Heifetz had the only five-and-ten-cent store, conducting business at the shop on the corner of First and Mount Avenues.

In addition to the Bay View, Hollywood, Lenox and Mandalay Inn hotels, another dozen property owners offered room and board, with Laura Litchfield advertising that her home at 24 Fourth Avenue particularly offered a "homelike place for vacationists."

The businesses were varied enough to include not only five automobile dealers but also an automobile painter; two bakeries; one bank; four barbers and two beauty parlors; two coal, wood and feed stores; two electricians; an employment agency; three garages and three hardware stores; nine insurance agencies; two jewelers; two laundries; and a machinist. There were also two places, the thriving Hopping McHenry and Frost business and a second shop, Atlantic Mason Supply, where one could purchase millwork and mason supplies, and four stores (including United Cigar, owned by William Leff) that sold newspapers and novelties. There were four tailors, two radio shops, four real estate agents, three restaurants (including the Log Cabin at the top of Ocean Boulevard), two tree surgeons and two photographers.

The Atlantic Highlands High School combined the eight preparatory grades with the four higher grades with instruction "conducted in a manner to ensure a high-class education for any and every pupil receiving its instruction."

The brochure concluded by promising that "Atlantic Highlands has every feature that makes living really worthwhile…beautiful scenery, perfect climate, abundant transportation, efficient utilities, picturesque homes, well-kept streets, shade trees under the care of the Shade Tree Commission, plentiful amusements, well tried religious and educational facilities…all of which are the desirable and necessary contributories to a happy American's home. And so, we say 'come and see for yourself the community that we are…'"

That was in the twentieth century; it's still true in the twenty-first. See for yourself!

—From the *Atlantic Highland Journal*, August 13, 2018

4

BOAT WORKS AND STREET FIGHTS

By Muriel J. Smith

Despite the efforts of Minnesota congressman Andrew J. Volstead and the Eighteenth Amendment to the Constitution, Prohibition was an exciting time in the Bayshore and an era remembered with both grief and good humor.

While the Volstead Act, which banned the sale of intoxicating liquors to anyone in the United States, was later recognized as a fourteen-year social experiment, it ended with the passage of the Twenty-First Amendment, which once again made it legal to buy alcohol.

Bill McCoy, a.k.a. the Real McCoy, remains one of the most popular rumrunners of the era, although there were others—families, clammers and fishermen whose names are inscribed in history or known only to their descendants through secretively handed-down stories—who profited during America's most far-reaching attempt to regulate morals.

Life changed along the rivers of Monmouth County during those fourteen years; fortunes were made, lives lost, families split apart and memories passed down for generations thereafter. Boatbuilders were suddenly much busier, sometimes building Coast Guard and rumrunner boats side by side. In Keyport, the Kofoed Boat Works had a reputation for fast, seaworthy sturdy skiffs—the kinds of boats that could make it three miles offshore to meet the other ships along Rum Row laden with illegal alcohol. Kofoed's forty-two-foot skiffs were powered by 190-horsepower Mianus engines and had a speed of twenty-two knots, even loaded with up to five hundred cases of liquor. When the Coast Guard ordered faster boats, Kofoed then built the "Wee" for their rumrunning customers, a fifty-foot skiff similar to the popular Sea Bright skiff also in service for both the Coast Guard and rumrunners. The Wee featured a broad, flat-bottomed transom and was powered by a pair of 400-horsepower Liberty engines.

The Jersey Skiff, often called the "Sports Car of the Water," is easily recognized and highly touted as a Jersey Shore invention and the most famous of all the boats built along the coast. In Highlands, Stewart King was one of the original builders of the skiff in the days when it was a wood lap strake construction with oak ribs all riveted together. King had more than two hundred patents for the skiff designs he and his family built at the King Boat Works on South Bay Avenue.

All along the Shrewsbury River, the Bayshore waterway that opened out to the Atlantic Ocean at the tip of Sandy Hook, the seafaring men who made their livings fishing, clamming, lobstering and boatbuilding by day became the bootleggers, rumrunners and smugglers who catered to the needs of a thirsty nation by night.

The age of the rumrunner was a lively time for Atlantic Highlands and Highlands, and it's still an exciting memory for the generation who can still hear the soft purr of high-speed boats, savor the taste of Usher's Green Stripe or Meyer's Perfection and utter the names of those revered rumrunners who plied the trade. It's still an exciting time for the families who know the locations of the tunnels that opened at the river's edge to provide safe havens for boats loaded with liquor. Some of those tunnels were

Twin Light Hotel, on the Shrewsbury River, was popular in Highlands during Prohibition. *Muriel J. Smith.*

connected to yet more secretive roadways farther up the hill, where waiting automobiles could be secretly loaded and sent on their way for deliveries throughout the state.

Respected smugglers, those who guaranteed unadulterated liquor, dealt with the highly esteemed wine, brandy and liquor shippers Maurice Meyer of London. The firm had been established in London in 1869 and was highly respected both in England and in the United States, where, during Prohibition, the firm only dealt—clandestinely—with respectable businessmen.

Meyer was certainly aware of Prohibition but also aware of the public's resentment of it, and the shippers knew there was a need they could capably and safely fulfill. So, the firm designed a series of codes that were used by smugglers and issued fictitious names and London addresses where orders could be sent. Buyers in the United States were then instructed to refer only to those code words and names in their cables and wires. This way, the anonymity of the smugglers—and the respected firm dealing with rumrunners—could be protected.

The specific codes were kind of fun, relating to flowers, fruits, vegetables or meats that were familiar to the bay men. Buchanan's Black and White Scotch, for instance, was known as roses; Hennessy's Three Star Brandy was apples. Even Moët & Chandon champagne was known by a different name (peaches), and gin was either salmon, mackerel or sole, depending on whether it was ordered in square or round bottles or casks.

But all of these entrepreneurs were dealing outside the law, which means that in addition to keeping out of reach of law enforcement, they also faced dangers and death from others engaging in their illegal trade—especially the hijackers, who made their livings by stealing from the bootleggers.

One of the more famous stories of the era was the Saturday night that ended in murder right in the heart of Atlantic Highlands. Apparently, according to a newspaper report from the day, hijacker Frank LeConte of Newark, regarded as the supreme leader in hijacking circles, had a row with Robert Schneider, a good old Highlands fellow successful in the running trade. Seems that a while before, LeConte's men interrupted what was going to be a successful delivery of goods by Schneider's men. This meant that there remained a score to settle.

When Schneider spotted LeConte in Highlands on this particular Saturday night, October 20, 1923, his men—led by Walter Keener and two sets of brothers, George and Henry Nettinger and Ed and Ralph Bitter—pursued the hijacker out of town. LeConte got a far as Center Avenue in Atlantic Highlands before, as luck would have it, he was forced to stop; there was a train halted in the station, blocking the road. As for the reason why LeConte was trapped, chalk it up to fate.

With no place to go and Schneider's men in hot pursuit, the only option was for LeConte and his associates to barrel out of their vehicles, weapons drawn, and let the gun battle begin.

It's said that LeConte was the first to be hit and was downed with a bullet in his stomach. Ralph Bitter took a shot to the shoulder, but it didn't stop him from carrying on the battle. When it was all over, LeConte and at least six others were treated for wounds at the hospital in Long Branch, and a whole handful on both sides were charged with various crimes.

LeConte didn't make it—he died in the hospital two days later. When it came down to the law assigning blame, the brothers Bitter were charged with LeConte's murder.

However, it didn't appear there were any witnesses—or, at least, there were no witnesses willing to tell the story of what happened that Saturday night on Center Avenue. There was no grand jury calling for an indictment. The brothers could return to plying their trade in Highlands.

—From the *Atlantic Highlands Herald*, July 6, 2017

5

HEROES ARE BURIED HERE

By Muriel J. Smith

Around Memorial Day, perhaps after the parade or before the backyard barbecue, or maybe in the evening before the sun sets—any time you might want to take a step back in history and see firsthand reasons for appreciating our military men and women, it might be a nice idea to take a stroll through Bay View Cemetery. There are more than three hundred people buried there who joined whatever forces were helping defend the United States at that time in their lives. Perhaps it's time to give special recognition to names that are still familiar in Monmouth County, like Stryker, Cassone, Luke and Swan, as well as those not so familiar, such as Rekzregel, Sory or Hay.

Hay—that's Fred Stewart Hay, or as his tombstone says, Frederick H. Schwabe. That's his small, plain white stone just beneath the U.S. flag as you enter the cemetery. By either name, Fred Hay or Frederick Schwabe is a hero. Our hero. More than that, he is a Medal of Honor recipient—one of just over 3,500 or so in the nation since it first honored heroism and bravery in the Civil War, and one of only 426 who earned the honor during the American Indian Wars, the series of conflicts that lasted from King Philip's War (at the end of the seventeenth century) through the next two centuries.

He served with Company I of the Fifth U.S. Infantry and rose to the rank of sergeant while serving. According to Medal of Honor records, he was born in 1850 in Stirlingshire, Scotland, and entered the U.S. Army at Fort Leavenworth, Kansas. At some point after his enlistment, Fred was in a small cavalry unit escorting a supply train to Battle Creek, where they were to meet up with General Nelson Miles's forces camped there. Miles, who had received his own Medal of Honor for action in the Civil War, was in desperate need of supplies and anxiously awaited the train at Battle Creek. On September 9, 1874, as the train came out of a canyon on the Upper Wachita River in what was then Texas (now Oklahoma), it was attacked by a large war party of Kiowa and Comanche warriors. Although they were heavily outnumbered, according to reports, the federal soldiers fought valiantly for an entire day, and the train successfully moved toward its destination. Hay, as a sergeant, was one of six men cited for their gallantry that day, with the commendation simply stating, "for gallantry," absent any other detail.

The battle continued for another two days, and in addition to Hay and the other five men who earned honors on the first day, another seven soldiers were also cited for their continuing efforts before the train finally reached the 650-man force and General Miles.

Sergeant Hay lived through the Civil War and for many years after, dying on January 14, 1914, at age sixty-four. When he came to Monmouth County, where he lived or why his family chose this serene, locally significant cemetery for his final resting place still remain mysteries. Medal of Honor records show the medal was issued to him at Upper Wichita, Texas, on September 9, 1874.

In fact, although his resting place is within the confines of Bay View Cemetery, the specific location of his remains is still unknown. Because of that, the Bay View Cemetery Association, wanting to be certain his memory is honored, thought it important that every visitor to Bay View Cemetery knows about the Medal of Honor recipient, so they placed his stone at the entrance. The tall U.S. flag that waves behind it is tended by the Atlantic Highlands American Legion and Veterans of Foreign Wars posts.

Captain George Porter is also buried at Bay View Cemetery. Captain Porter fought at the Battle of Mobile under Admiral Farragut during the Civil War and had begun his career in the navy as a signal boy, a title considered so important that it is engraved on his tombstone. Right up there with his rank of captain is the notation, "the only signal boy in the US Navy."

William Sory is probably not the only Confederate soldier buried at Bay View Cemetery. Born in Virginia, Sory was a private in the Confederate States Army, Company G, part of the Virginia Infantry. One wonders what brought a Confederate to the North to finish out the rest of his life after battling those who lived here. Retired cemetery manager Walter Curry said it is believed there are some other Confederate military members who fought for the South also interred at Bay View. The list goes on, and each veteran's story is important, whether it is known or committed to the ages.

The cemetery itself has a fascinating history as a well-cared-for, beloved resting place for generations of families from the Highlands, Atlantic Highlands, Leonardo, Navesink, Belford and Chapel Hill areas. It started, according to author Thomas Leonard, in his ancestor's law office in 1889, when a group of residents saw the need for a burial ground and formed a company to purchase the land. Attorney Leonard became the secretary of the first company, with former Judge George H. Sickles serving as the chairman of the new Bay View Land Improvement Company, Ltd. The cemetery association was organized, and fifty-two acres of land carved from R.A. Leonard's farm were purchased for a total of $13,300. Each of the partners agreed to purchase a lot in the cemetery, and that was the first money raised for maintaining and improving the land.

A quiet, thoughtful visit to the cemetery gives one time and opportunity to think about the men and women buried there—not only the veterans but other ancestors of families who still take pride in calling the Bayshore home. Take a good look at the names on the gravestones—names that still resonate. Look for the final resting place of Mayor Everett Curry, who tended this cemetery for so many years before his son Walter took up the mantle. Both of the Currys seemed to be on a first-name basis with all who are buried there, with Everett lovingly tending the graves for twenty years, until 1994, before his son (and also a former Atlantic Highlands council member) Walter Curry came on board as an assistant in 1978, then assumed the full-time manager position in 2000.

—From the *Atlantic Highlands Herald*, May 26, 2016

6

HIGHLANDS TRIBUTE TO COOPER'S *WATER WITCH*

by Muriel J. Smith

With all the references to James Fenimore Cooper's book *The Water Witch* among the streets in Highlands (Seadrift Avenue, Waterwitch Avenue, the Waterwitch section of the Boro, Barberie Avenue), we might sometimes forget that there's another street in neighboring Atlantic Highlands named after another character from the book: Beverout Place. Former mayor Dick Stryker reminded us of that story, which is as fascinating as Lust-in-Rust itself.

What's more, there were other U.S. Navy ships named *Water Witch*, one of which later became the CSS *Water Witch*!

Lust-in-Rust was the name Cooper gave to an actual country estate located in the hills of Highlands. It was built by Esek Hartshorne in the 1700s and featured a massive brick fireplace and chimney, both of which survived a fire and the elements through the twentieth century. In his book, Cooper called it Rust-in-Lust, although historians do not know why the author chose that name. Cooper's Myndert Van Beverout was a fictitious wealthy fur merchant and New York city official who owned the estate. It was Beverout who was buying all those silks and other magnificent luxuries from Tom Tiller, the mystery man on the *Water Witch*, the ship used for smuggling and other excitement and affairs throughout the book. The ship itself was named for its figurehead, a not very pretty but indeed very ominous-looking water witch. It was British naval officer Captain Cornelius Ludlow and the HMS *Coquette* who had made it their mission to capture the smuggling ship *Water Witch* and put an end to its activities at sea and in the ports up and down the coastline.

The love interest in the book—there's always a love interest in novels set in the eighteenth century—is Beverout's beautiful niece, the Lady Barberie, or, to be perfectly proper, Alida de Barbérie. She suddenly vanished after one of those negotiating sessions over silks and things, and it became known she was on the *Water Witch* with the very handsome captain, Master Seadrift.

The rest of Cooper's novel details the chase and sea battles around Sandy Hook and Long Island until the ending, when the reader learns who marries whom, who's in love with whom and what happens to the *Water Witch*. Beverout's name remains famous on a street named in his honor in the hills of Atlantic Highlands!

While the book does not have the excitement and easy readability of twenty-first-century novels, it's one of Cooper's lighter works, and reviewers have noted that in spite of the very authentic sea chases and sailing adventures, it is a book filled with whimsy.

Cooper wrote the book in Naples, Italy, a place the author considered to be the most beautiful of any he had seen around the world. He stayed many months there in the 1820s, enjoying life with his wife and children during what appears to be the happiest time in his life. Yet, while he drank in the beauty and charm of the Bay of Naples and Sorrento itself, strangely enough, he set the book in the Sandy Hook Bay and New York area around the beginning of the eighteenth century, which only proves that no matter where you are, no matter how magnificent the setting, there's something so special about the Bayshore that makes you always want to be a part of it.

As for the *Water Witch*, there were, in actuality, three real ships in the U.S. Navy with that name, with the most famous being the one built in the 1850s and launched at the Naval Yard in Washington, D.C. It was in and out of service for a few years—used to conduct surveys of South American coastlines and rivers before the Civil War, then as a delivery ship after the Confederate attack at Fort Sumter, carrying mail and messages through the blockade between there and Key West. After achieving success on that mission, it was on yet another mission a couple of years later when it was boarded and captured by the Confederate navy, which kept the vessel's name the same. Thus, it became the CSS *Water Witch*. It was used by the Confederates until nearly the end of the Civil War, when it was burned to prevent it being recaptured by the Union. There is a full-scale reproduction of the wooden-hulled steamer at the National Civil War Naval Museum in Columbus, Georgia. The museum also is home to the original bell from the ship, one of its flags and a Bible, all taken from the ship before it was destroyed.

—From the *Atlantic Highlands Herald*, May 8, 2017

7

THE SEARCH FOR HIGHLANDS WORLD WAR II CASUALTIES

By Rick Geffken

It's easy to miss the small white stone nestled between the flagpoles at Veterans Memorial Park in Highlands. The small hill rising near the Shrewsbury River is dominated by a tribute to thousands of 9/11 victims: two imposing bas-relief sculptures and four engraved boulders. If you happen upon the small white stone, you'll see a bronze plaque inscribed with these few words: "Dedicated to those who made the Supreme Sacrifice in World War II." The names of thirteen Highlands men who died during that long-ago conflict follow that solemn inscription.

This unimposing monument to a few deceased veterans did not escape the notice of Walt Guenther of the Historical Society of Highlands. The stone was originally in Huddy Park in the Water Witch section of town before it was moved to the park on the corner of Bay and Shrewsbury Avenues. Guenther believes the stories of these memorialized patriots deserve to be remembered today, seventy-one years after the fighting stopped.

Guenther has been a summer resident of Highlands for his entire life, continuing the family tradition spanning almost one hundred years. They moved into their summer bungalow on Marine Place in the Borough in 1943.

"As I was growing up, it seemed like all the older Highlands men were vets in those days," Guenther says. "We played Army as kids and ran around in all our parks. I walked right by these names but didn't know anything about them."

After attending Cornell University and enjoying a career in corporate finance, Guenther settled in Ohio with his wife and children. They returned to Highlands every summer to spend time with his grown siblings and their parents. A few years ago, he joined the local historical society, of which his parents had been charter members. When he asked other members about the names on the World War II plaque, he was surprised to find that very little was known about them. "I've always respected vets, though I'm not one myself," he says. "They gave their lives for our country, and we ought to know as much as we can about them." Thus, Guenther began his search to honor the service of the forgotten men.

Walt estimated that at least three generations have passed since World War II, and it was unlikely any of the parents of the thirteen men were still alive. Who else might know about them? Remaining relatives might not often think about the men who were shipped off to the Pacific or Europe in the 1940s. Sad memories fade, people move away, old photographs and letters molder away in attics or basements. Maybe some of these servicemen were just summer residents, or even unmarried, and therefore would have had no family connections at all in the Highlands.

Guenther visited the Highlands VFW and the American Legion Post to inquire about the names on the stone. "Nobody seemed to know. Same story when I went to town hall." However, he did discover that 265 men and 5 women from Highlands volunteered or were drafted for military service. "Thirteen deaths out of two hundred and seventy seemed pretty high to me," he recalls. He started digging into online resources like census records and newspapers. Contacting family members of some of the fallen heroes turned out to be a great source of information. Obituaries for a few of the names yielded tiny biographical details. He found that all thirteen were enlisted men—not one was an officer. One particularly heroic story emerged from Guenther's investigations; that story revealed a Highlands family devastated by two tragedies.

Try as he might, Guenther could not find any military records for Ernest Arnath, who died while serving in the navy. By cross-checking the last name, Guenther found that the man's first name had been incorrectly transcribed. He was *Eugene* Arnath, and he was a decorated hero. Arnath was a seaman on the submarine USS *Sculpin* patrolling the waters near Truk Island in the South Pacific in 1943. When a Japanese destroyer discovered the sub, it was subjected to a withering twelve-hour depth charge attack. Forced to surface, the submariners were easy targets for the destroyer's guns. The American crew scrambled to defend themselves. Eugene Arnath returned many rounds of fire from the sub's deck gun until he was hit and killed. His heroism was rewarded with a Bronze Star. Many of his shipmates were killed, while a lucky few were captured.

We can only imagine the devastation of Arnath's mother, Clara Bloodgood Rugg Arnath, when she received the awful news back in Highlands. Her grief was compounded when, less than a year after Eugene's loss, one of her sons from a previous marriage, Charles Rugg, was also killed in combat.

Rugg was a rifleman with the U.S. Army's Twenty-Ninth Infantry, one of the battalions that stormed Normandy Beach in France. Though he hasn't yet discovered exactly where Charles Rugg died, Guenther believes Rugg made it off that beach during the famous invasion of 1944 but was cut down farther inland just a few weeks later. Rugg's remains are with thousands of his comrades in arms in the U.S. Military Cemetery in Normandy. Guenther doesn't know if Clara Arnath, a two-time Gold Star mother (the designation used for women who lost sons during the war), was ever able to visit Charles's gravesite.

At a June meeting of the Historical Society of Highlands at the new community center, Guenther revealed the personal stories of these men and the seven other deceased soldiers and sailors he has researched. Each man deserves mention here:

- Samuel Parker (U.S. Coast Guard), lost at sea in the North Atlantic in 1942
- George "Red" Hauber (U.S. Navy), died during Battle of Santa Cruz, Solomon Islands, 1942
- Michael "Oats" Patterson, killed in North Africa, 1943
- Willard Robertson (U.S. Army), tank battalion trooper, died in Normandy in 1944
- Lewis Mount (U.S. Army), killed during tank battle in France, 1944
- Edward Minor (U.S. Navy), salvage diver, lost off Norfolk, Virginia, in 1945
- Robert Matthews (U.S. Navy), aviation mechanic, MIA from aircraft carrier in January 1946 (yes, records state his death as after the official armistice)

Guenther is not discouraged that he has uncovered precious little information about the other four men listed on the stone: Leroy Smith, John M. Greene, Kenneth Furey and John Ryan Jr. The very evening of his talk, a historical society member mentioned she knew relatives of one of the deceased men. Someone else gave him a newspaper article with promising leads to follow.

"Maybe someone who reads about this in the *Two River Times* will recall something, too. Or might recognize a last name associated with Highlands in those days," Guenther says, optimistically. Guenther is determined to pursue and publish the stories of these young, brave men.

Walt Guenther intends to write a full report on the background stories of all thirteen men for the Historical Society of Highlands. President Russell Card is confident it will be a valuable document for the society's archives and all borough residents: "Walt found out so much in such a short time, I just know he'll do a comprehensive job."

Walt plans to record all he finds on a compact disc and maybe even author a book on the contributions of the men from this small town. "I'm going to give copies to the VFW and American Legion. A couple of generations from now, they won't have to start from scratch for information on these brave guys."

—From the *Two River Times*, July 28–August 4, 2016

HIGHLANDS VIETNAM WAR HERO

By Muriel J. Smith

They buried Tommy Ptak Monday morning, the *Highlands Star*, the local newspaper in Highlands, reported on April 4, 1968.

It was Specialist Fourth Class Thomas Ptak, a resident of 270 Highland Avenue, son of Mr. and Mrs. Benjamin Ptak, to the very militarily correct army sergeant who escorted the soldier's body from the place where he died in Hue, Vietnam, back home to Highlands for the funeral, then on to Mount Olivet Cemetery, where he will rest forever.

It was Specialist Thomas Ptak to the six ramrod-straight and army-perfect soldiers who served as pallbearers at the military funeral at Our Lady of Perpetual Help Church, where Tommy and his family had worshiped all his life—the church where he had been baptized, the church where he received his First Communion (and many more Communions after that), the church where priests heard his confessions would now be the church where a Mass was being offered to honor his death.

To all Americans, to all citizens of a free country, it was Specialist Thomas Ptak whose body lay in the plain casket under the U.S. flag.

But to the hundreds of people who crowded into Our Lady of Perpetual Help Church for a last goodbye and a funeral Mass and the dozens more who spilled out onto the steps of the church that has a spectacular view of the Atlantic Ocean, it was just plain Tommy. It was Tommy to his young brothers and sisters, some of whom weren't old enough to comprehend the ugly way in which he died. It was Tommy to his sorrowing parents, who couldn't begin to comprehend what wonderful guides they had been and

Thomas Ptak was the only Highlands native who died in the Vietnam War. *William Ptak.*

how much love they received from all ten of their children. It was Tommy, the son who would have been proud of their strength at his funeral.

It was Tommy to the dozens and dozens of high school students from the regional high school he attended and the two local Catholic high schools that some of his friends attended. They all could remember happier days, when Tommy was skillfully performing on a gym horse or tossing a ball with them in the middle of the street.

It was Tommy to the school principals who remembered Tommy as a "good boy, a typical boy, the kind you'd want in any class." It was Tommy to practically every neighbor along Highland Avenue and Valley Street, where Tommy grew up, folks who remembered a friendly wave or a smile from a busy youth working on a motorcycle in the yard as they passed the always-happy, always-busy Ptak home. These neighbors had broken all the rules of protocol and flew their flags at half-staff even before Highlands mayor John A. Bahrs ordered it for the entire town. These neighbors had all gone out to their front yards to lower their flags the minute they heard of Tommy's death.

It was Tommy to the three priests who concelebrated the funeral Mass: the one who grew up in the parish and knew the whole Ptak family, the one who spent five years in the parish and knew and visited often with the family and the one who had just arrived in Highlands the previous year and was not lucky enough to get closely acquainted with the young hero.

It was Tommy to the police chief and members of the police department who could remember he was "a nice kid; we ought to have more like him."

It was Tommy to the altar boys who formed their own guard of honor as his body left the church, boys who were classmates of Tommy's younger brothers or sisters at the parochial school next to the church—the school Tommy had also attended.

It was Tommy to the grammar school girls who sorrowfully sang a very special funeral Mass. It was a Mass for the Tommy some of them had looked up to when they were very small, and he was a big eighth-grader. It was Tommy, the big brother of their classmates, the big brother who looked so grown up and handsome in his army uniform.

It was Tommy to a neighbor who had spent more than twenty years in the service of his country. Now retired as a sergeant major, Sal Giovenco attended the funeral in full dress uniform, perhaps to show the family of the young hero that he was proud of this particular soldier, proud to have known him and proud to show that he, too, believes in the cause for which Tommy died. Sal knew—and showed—that Tommy deserved the honor and respect of the American soldier's uniform.

The official records refer to Tommy as Thomas John Ptak. Born February 1, 1948, died March 22, 1968. Army records indicate he was an E4, Specialist Fourth Class, ID No. 11755688, a member of C Company, Second Battalion, 501st Infantry, 101st Infantry Regiment (Geronimo, as it was known). He started his Vietnam tour on December 14, 1967, and he was in Thua Thien province in South Vietnam on March 22, 1968, ninety-eight days later, when he was killed in a hostile ground attack of multiple fragmentation wounds. He died outright, the records say. His body was recovered. He had many honors—the Purple Heart, Good Conduct Medal, National Defense Medal, Combat Infantry Badge and several Vietnam Campaign Medals presented by the South Vietnamese government in appreciation for the U.S. forces.

They buried Tommy Ptak Monday morning, the newspaper continued. The nation lost a soldier, parents lost a son and Highlands lost a very special youth.

Tommy Ptak was the town's only casualty of the Vietnam War. It was as a tribute to him and to the cause for which he fought that the borough's first high-rise senior citizen complex, located just down the hill from where he worshipped, was dedicated as Ptak Towers.

Tommy Ptak would love that the borough's first affordable housing built to help the older residents of the town he loved so much stands as a living memorial to him.

—From the *Middletown Courier*, April 8, 1968

9

MOUNT MITCHILL IN BEAUTY, SPLENDOR AND TRIBUTE

By Muriel J. Smith

In September 2001, it was the open field that drew hundreds of residents who didn't want to witness—but somehow had to see—the devastation across the water and the collapse of the Twin Towers. At the highest point on the waterfront, crowds gathered to gasp at the devastation, the smoke billowing in the air, the ferries crossing Sandy Hook Bay to bring victims—some with injuries, most in shock—to the safety of the more protected docks in Highlands and Atlantic Highlands, far from the inferno.

Since that day, every September 11, Mount Mitchill has also drawn contemplative crowds that gather for the Monmouth County Park System's annual commemoration. Local freeholders, legislators, mayors, military, clergy, scouts, volunteers and administrators from all levels of government join hands with children, couples and families, all with their own memories, and offer silent tribute to those who lost their lives at the World Trade Center.

That awful day is poignantly commemorated at Mount Mitchill with the sculpture of a bald eagle with a piece of the World Trade Center carnage clutched in its talons and a memorial citing each of the 147 Monmouth County residents who lost their lives that September day.

The sculpture was created by Italian-born New Jersey sculptor Franco Minervini, whose work also graces the Washington National Cathedral, among many other historic locations. A natural sculptor in his hometown of Molfetta, Italy, Minervini later studied and worked for five years under noted sculptor Vincent Palumbo and studied sculpture at the New School in New York.

But even before the World Trade Center fell, even before the devastation, Mount Mitchill was a special place. Undisputedly, this is the highest land along the Atlantic Seaboard from Maine to the Yucatan—if you don't count an island off of Maine. Standing 266 feet tall, the mount's amazing height can best be attributed to the effects of glacial rebound. Ages-old ironstone conglomerate created a caprock along the crest overlying marine mud rocks. When the sea level was lower (many centuries ago), the Highlands hills were a high valley wall on the south side of the Hudson and Raritan Rivers. The river system was later buried by younger sediments, including deposits from the Sandy Hook Spit.

In addition to its high perch along Sandy Hook Bay, which ultimately opens out to the Atlantic Ocean, Mount Mitchill stands out for its history and natural beauty as well as its contemplative area recalling 9/11 and quiet recreation area for the younger generation (once it became a county park).

There was a time in the twentieth century when the land was going to be the site of a ten-story apartment house that would have been a twin to equal the high-rise on the adjacent Highlands side of the crest. Stories of slump blocks, the hill falling and, most importantly, the will of the people kept the construction from happening. The Monmouth County Park System acquired the land in 1973, making the twelve-acre site one of forty-three county owned parks. In 1980, it became a memorial to the Iran hostage crisis; the flagpole on the parkland is dedicated to the fifty-two American hostages who were held captive for 444 days. The eight-sided plaque beneath the flag pays tribute to the eight military men who gave their lives in an unsuccessful attempt to rescue the captives.

Mount Mitchill was named for Samuel Latham Mitchill, an eighteenth- and nineteenth-century physician, naturalist, lawyer and politician who earned his medical degree in Scotland and taught chemistry and natural history at Columbia College (as the present-day university was known in the 1790s). He also collected, identified and classified plants, animals and aquatic organisms for his studies and, in the 1820s, was an organizer of the medical college at Rutgers, where he served as vice president and was an early advocate of personal hygiene and sanitation as powerful means to prevent disease.

But he was even more than that, this Long Island–born gentleman whose curiosity led him to expand his knowledge in numerous fields and disciplines. He served as a New York state legislator, a U.S. senator and—both before and after that term—as a congressman. He was a strong supporter and advocate of building the Erie Canal. It is not surprising that he was an ardent fan of Thomas Jefferson, who apparently admired him as well, since the third president referred to him as the "Congressional Dictionary."

While it is not clear why the highest point on the waterfront is named for Mitchill, there is much speculation. Perhaps it was his connection to Rutgers University or his vast contributions to science and ecology, or perhaps he could see the heights from his Long Island home and felt a connection; perhaps it was the result of the respect he earned in both political and scientific circles.

Whatever the reason for its moniker, Monmouth County's Mount Mitchill stands as a tribute to history, bravery, an attack on the United States and a scientist and politician who died in New York in 1831. Samuel Latham Mitchill is buried at Greenwood Cemetery in New York.

—From the *Atlantic Highlands Herald*, September 22, 2016

10

The Hills Are Alive with the Sound of History

By Rick Geffken

When Sallie Adams and Tom Kaiser started looking around Monmouth County for a new home in 1994, they were less interested in the area's rich history than in finding a tranquil setting for their family. The well-traveled couple and their sons loved Manhattan but needed a change. Several months of exploring real estate listings in the Two Rivers area didn't yield a house that excited them.

"We'd almost given up thoughts of moving," Sallie says, when their real estate agent Columbo-ed: "There's just one more thing." He talked them into visiting the Monmouth Hills section of Middletown to look at a "cottage."

After turning off Highway 36 onto the well-hidden Serpentine Drive, Sallie and Tom scarcely believed they were so close to the shore. Was it possible that this enclave, so close to a major highway artery, was filled with so many charming and distinctive homes and rustic lanes winding in and out of the woods?

By the time they reached "Sea Vista" on East Twin Road, they were amazed at their luck. The Shingle-style house with sawtooth cedar shake filigree, the several unenclosed eves and the exposed roof rafters enchanted them. The house had spectacular ocean and bay views from every window, lots of open space, three working fireplaces and a former horse stable on the ground floor—who had read their minds? Wouldn't their boys just love the quirky sleeping porch extension from the master bedroom and the mysterious second-floor "door to nowhere"? The five-minute ride to the Seastreak Ferry dock was a delightful bonus. Sold!

One hundred years before, an earlier generation of New Yorkers was equally intrigued by the hurly-burly going on in the Highlands of Navesink. On summer weekends during the last decade of the nineteenth century, boarding houses, hotels, tents, bungalows and boats in the little clamming and fishing community on the Shrewsbury River were filled to capacity. It caught the attention of the *New York Times*, which proclaimed: "Highland Beach has features, perhaps, that no other resort on the Atlantic coast possesses."

It wasn't unusual for ten thousand people—per day—to flood the runaway success that was William Sandlass's five-year-old excursion resort. Day trippers came by steamship and train to enjoy ocean and river bathing, merry-go-round rides, strolls along the boardwalk, seaside restaurants and ice cream and soda shops—all to escape the city heat and their workaday lives.

Inevitably, this excitement caused a flurry of building in the Highlands. New homes and estates were creeping up to the castle-like Twin Lights on Mount Mitchill, the highest point on the Eastern Seaboard from Maine to Florida. A part of that 240-foot hillside in what was then called Sea Side offered unparalleled views of Sandy Hook, Coney Island and beyond—all the way to New York City.

The prominent investor behind the development of Highland Beach was the New York real estate magnate Ferdinand Fish. Fish, who was delighted as his plans for the development of the area started to bear fruit, next organized the Highlands of Navesink Improvement Company, recruiting wealthy leisure-class friends. The resulting Water Witch Club aimed for a limited number of high-design homes in a sylvan setting for kindred spirits. Fish knew the perfect place to create a special social environment for folks with money and artistic leanings.

The Water Witch Club purchased a huge tract on Mount Mitchill, including an extensive area down to the Shrewsbury River. The club's name was homage to James Fenimore Cooper's 1830 novel *The Water Witch*, which has long been associated with the small bayside community.

As head draftsman for the Beaux Arts architectural firm Carrère and Hastings, Lyman A. Ford was on the team that won the competition to design the New York Public Library in 1897. A year later, Ford was assigned to design and build houses in the new and exclusive colony on Mount Mitchill. He built at least six, including his own Sea Vista. Of course, he picked the best spot on the hill for his summer home just a short walk from the Casino clubhouse.

Water Witch Club homeowners took their meals at the Casino in the early years of the community—no one wanted heat-generating kitchens inside summer cottages. The Casino, which was the center of the elite's social life of games, recitals and dances, was not a gambling venue, as the name implies today, but was more like a clubhouse for various social events.

When a fire destroyed the Casino in 1911, Lyman Ford designed a replacement, the only private "casino" (now used for weddings and other social events) remaining in New Jersey; it is listed in the National Register of Historic Places. Ford's interior motif of rich, dark wood was highlighted by an elevated stage for plays and other Water Witch Club productions. A dining room, sitting room and five upstairs bedrooms accommodated the steady stream of summer guests at the little colony. Tennis courts and a sweeping lawn overlooking Sandy Hook Bay and the ocean enhanced this idyllic playground. In 1916, the community officially changed its name to Monmouth Hills. Abandoning the private club concept, "the Hills" morphed into a nonprofit homeowners' association.

In recent years, Sallie Adams and Tom Kaiser's good neighbor, Mary Jo Kenny, related the history of Sea Vista and Monmouth Hills, where she's lived for over forty years. As president of the Twin Lights Historical Society, she has amassed an archive of documents, photos, letters and the like. Kenny related the story of that odd door in Sea Vista. "During the Second World War, when housing was scarce for people working to support our troops at Fort Hancock on Sandy Hook, Sea Vista was divided into up and down apartments, each with its own entrance. When it was reconverted to a one-family residence, the second-floor stairway was dismantled, but the door was left in place, still workable." Soon after, a wrought iron gate was added outside the door to prevent unintended exits. It's a cool and quirky feature.

Lyman Ford lived in Sea Vista for forty-five years. Sallie and Tom's time there will be about half of Ford's—a country home in Virginia beckons them. They've recently decided to sell Sea Vista, the only one of the Lyman Ford–built cottages left. Improvements during their stay include a modern kitchen, an entertainment room in the former stable area and landscaping to beautify the setting. The couple kept the look and feel of this nineteenth-century gem, even replicating period wallpaper in several rooms. Yes, the "door to nowhere" is still there.

Sallie Adams and Tom Kaiser were looking for just the right buyer—someone who appreciates the unique history of Highlands and Middletown, someone with an artistic imagination like Lyman Ford's, someone who wants to see for miles and miles…and someone who will love a Sea Vista.

—From the *Two River Times*, July 7, 2016

II

The Fire Department at NWS Earle

By Muriel J. Smith

Less than two months after the Naval Ammunition Depot Earle (NAD Earle) was established in New Jersey, during the heart of World War II, the U.S. Navy, in addition to building a small city of homes, shops, a post office, paved streets, office buildings, recreation facilities and water, electric, fuel, heating and transportation supplies, also had a thriving fire department. It became the first—and only—installation of the navy to be named after a person rather than the city in which it is located. Named after Rear Admiral Ralph A. Earle, the chief of the Bureau of Ordnance during World War I, the base's location was frequently given as Earle, New Jersey. In actuality, it spreads over four different communities: Middletown, Colts Neck, Ocean Township and Tinton Falls.

It was in February 1944 that the new depot—the only one of its kind in the world—had a civilian, C.W. Clayton, as its first fire chief.

Chief Clayton began his career at the naval facility with one American LaFrance pumper truck, one American LaFrance assembly army 6X6 MC truck with a Chrysler-driven Hale single-stage five-hundred-gallons-per-minute pumping unit, and an American LaFrance–assembled five-hundred-gallons-per-minute pumping unit mounted on a Ford chassis. Each was equipped with the essentials: suction hose, strainers, ladders and a few extinguishers. Water hoses, tools and firefighting equipment were still to come. The chief had four marines assigned to the new department—two for the station in Colts Neck, the main part of the base, and two in Leonardo, at the very busy pier area. The Ford chassis pumper was dispatched to the pier, the others to the main side.

With construction ongoing at the beginning of 1944, the fire station was still waiting for the water system to be installed and wells to be driven. The only water available was through the lines the contractors had laid for building and sanitation purposes for the workers. The pumping units often had to wait until after the day's work was done to refill their tanks.

There was a garage on the Colts Neck side of the base that was big enough for one unit. It was still winter, so oil stoves were used to keep the water in the tank and lines from freezing. On the pier side, there was a fire headquarters on an improvised road into the meadows, and all booster lines were drained to avoid freezing. Water to refill the tanks came from the local water provider for the nearby communities.

The navy was working quickly and efficiently to complete construction; a squad of ten marines was added to the department to be trained in firefighting and to respond to fire alarms that came through the corporal of the guard by phone or radio, then to the fire department. The marines trained long and hard, and by March, it was well set as a strong and efficient firefighting unit. By April, the fire house was finished, and water mains were installed and fed by an artesian well, although at the pier, the tie-in still had to be made through the local water company. Another six marines were dispatched to fire duty, with all sixteen marines taking on fire protection in addition to their regular duties. They served as drivers, telephone contacts, pump operators and firefighters. The following month, twenty-three sailors were added to the detail, all enlisted, drilled, schooled and trained in firefighting. Seven served on the pier, and the other sixteen were assigned to the main side. The department was growing, maintaining its streamlined efficiency. The men were following a rigid training schedule every other day, a round-the-clock desk watch was established at the pier and a fire saltwater system, with hose installation and trained working parties, was built on one of the piers in order to take advantage of the natural river water supply.

The first major fire call was on May 29, 1944: a garage fire in a remote area on the east side of the Colts Neck portion. The alarm had been delayed, but once it was received, the firefighters responded to the scene in less than four minutes. Already, the building was engulfed, with all sides bursting in flame. The garage was fifty feet from a large above-ground tank where twenty thousand gallons of gasoline and fuel oil were stored. There were no water mains to the remote area, so water came by tank trucks to the fire apparatus and barrels at the scene. Records indicate that twenty thousand gallons of water were used to quell the fire. The determination, skill and training of the marines and sailors paid off; although the garage was gone, the firefighters kept the fire from spreading, and the storage tank—with its supply of flammable liquids—was saved.

Improvements continued to be made to the fire department throughout the year. Military members and firefighters drew their own conclusion: during the planning and construction of the piers, buildings and all other areas, fire protection did not seem to be a major consideration. However, the young, newly trained department members were not fazed. Six portable pumping units were added to the Navy Barge Pier (later called the Army and Navy piers), a twenty-four-hour watch was set up for each pump and an assistant fire chief was added to the payroll to take over responsibility of the pier area and lessen the load on the fire chief. By the end of 1944, just a year after Naval Ammunition Depot had become a reality and a major force during World War II, the department had ninety-six enlisted military men, a chief, an assistant chief and two civilian fire inspectors. They owned eight pieces of mobile firefighting equipment, fourteen trailer pumping units and one stationary pumping station. At the time, it was considered to be one of the best-equipped, best-trained and best-kept departments in the navy's complete complement of shore establishments. In their first year, the department answered a total of 133 calls—98 at the Colts Neck side and 35 at the pier area. There were no serious or major damages and no recorded injuries.

At the end of 1944, it was still a month or so before the first African American woman was permitted to join the navy. It was a few months before the Marine Corps had its first African American officer. And it was nearly four years before President Harry S. Truman signed Executive Order 9981 that abolished discrimination in the military and led to the end of segregated troops.

But at NAD Earle, officials' historic records show: "In the past 16 months, the Fire Chief found not the slightest differences between Marines and colored sailors or civil personnel and found that they coordinate their efforts for the war effort, the Navy and NAD Fire Departments to excess."

With Lieutenant Harold A. Lindecker, the fire marshal of the depot, and Lieutenant Colonel Gannon, USMC, at the helm, together with depot civilians and enlisted men, NAD Earle proved it was way ahead of its time then and now.

—Previously unpublished

12

Nellie McHenry, a Stage Star Living in Highlands

By Muriel J. Smith

While Highlands has always been an area that movie stars, journalists like Jim Bishop, television personalities and entertainers like to call home because of its serenity and natural beauty, it had more than its share of popular stars of the stage and screen in the late nineteenth and early twentieth centuries. Nellie McHenry Webster was just one of those famous names.

Known professionally as Nellie McHenry, she was born in St. Louis, Missouri, and toured the country, as well as Canada, with other stage stars like Edwin Booth and Lillian Russell. She began her career in her native city but went on to Chicago, where she performed with the Hooley Comedy Company. She met John Webster, whom she later married, and Nate Salsbury, a theatrical impresario, and the trio formed the Salisbury Troubadors, who toured for nearly twenty years in the 1870s and 1880s.

It was Salsbury, who also lived in Highlands, who organized actors into a small series of plays joined with a single thread of a plot—an idea that was hugely successful and led to the troupe, Nellie included, going to Australia and Tasmania, of all places, to display their talent. The Troubadors disbanded around 1890, but Salsbury kept things alive as co-owner of the Buffalo Bill Wild West Show, which went on to earn even greater acclaim.

Nellie toured numerous countries in Europe as well, bringing her stage talent to the public through her expertise in both comedy and drama. At one time, in the 1880s, she had a week's engagement at the Chestnut Street

Theater in Philadelphia, and many extras were needed for minor roles at those performances. They were provided by none other than J.S. Hoffman, who also happened to be a Highlands councilman in 1935 at the time of her death.

Nellie and her husband had their home atop the hill on Portland Road, a gracious old Victorian with massive porches on two levels to ensure constant views of the Shrewsbury River and Atlantic Ocean. Salsbury also lived in the area, as did Wallace Reed and Franchon Campbell Webster, Nellie's daughter, who, like Nellie's son, John Jr., made her living on stage and was a highly regarded actress.

After starring in *M'Liss* and finding huge success with that one-act play, Nellie bought the rights to the play, then conducted her own highly successful tour around the country with it.

Nellie died at Monmouth Medical Center (then known as Hazard Hospital), in Long Branch, when she was eighty-two years old. Her funeral was at the A.M. Posten Funeral Home in Atlantic Highlands, and the service was held at All Saints Memorial Church in Locust, with the rector, Reverend Charles P. Johnson, officiating. She is buried in the church cemetery.

Her husband, John Webster, disappeared one night in 1899, and it is believed he committed suicide by jumping into the rapids at Niagara Falls. His body has never been found. Their son, John Jr., died of a heart attack in 1925 in his dressing room at the Henry Miller Theater on West Forty-Third Street, in New York City, just a scarce few minutes before his curtain call for the play *The Poor Nut*.

—From the *Atlantic Highlands Herald*, April 19, 2018

13

POLICE CHECKED LIGHTS AND LOCKED DOORS IN THE 1930s

By Muriel J. Smith

It just takes scanning some old police logs for the borough of Highlands to see how life in this terrific town was a bit easier in the earlier part of the twentieth century. It was a bit more laid-back, overflowing with kindness and wonderful people who helped each other and took a lot of bad times in stride.

It was also a time when our local men in blue had different duties and responsibilities than today's police department. While praise and appreciation can be heaped on the fine men and women who protect this town today under great leadership and dedication, it's fun to look at some of the logbooks from 1930 and see so many of the names that were part of the community then are still very much memorable and a part of Highlands in the twenty-first century.

Howard Brey—the first one, not the chief from the latter part of the twentieth century—was an officer then, as were Kyril Parker, Howard Johnson and William Lawrence. Howard Monahan, also a police officer at that time, later became chief of police in the 1960s. The officers kept their logs neatly handwritten and very specific in regard to time, not only for door inspections and general patrol but also for a forty-five-minute lunch period and streetlight inspections.

When it came to death and accidents, they are all devoid of any emotionalism. Nor are the logs replete with any investigatory detail.

Prohibition was in effect in the early 1930s, there was an active army base at Fort Hancock and one of the nightly duties of the officer on patrol was to check streetlights. So, the log is full of notations about specific streetlights not being operable, including one at the corner of Marine Place and Waterwitch, Light No. 28 on Navesink Avenue, and No. 1 light on Highland Avenue. There are no reports about whether the light outages were ever reported elsewhere or reinstated.

Police also did regular door checks and immediately took care of small problems, as when Officer Parker "found Ned Catton's store door locked, and the key was in the lock. So, I brought it back to headquarters."

The same thing happened a few days later at Frank Hall's store, where the key was also in the lock; the officer turned the key and brought it back to headquarters for the storekeeper to pick up the next morning.

It was also a time when people reported everything, big or small, whether it was significant to the entire community or just helping out a single person. The police took care of it all. For instance, the August 31, 1930 log written by Patrol Officer Brey shows that at 11:00 p.m. that night, "Mr. Ed LaRue of 2nd St. reported the awning on the Bay Ave. side of Wagner's Meat Market was hanging very low and it should be raised up as Edward Duncan of 2nd St. did not notice it and walked into it receiving a cut over his eye. I [Officer Brey] went to Morris Schwartz store at Bay Avenue and Miller St. and got the handle that he had so I could raise the awning."

A little later that same night, Patrol Officer Parker wrote, "While trying store doors I discovered a man on the avenue sick with pain in stomach. I took him to Doctor Rowland, he examined the man and told me to take him

Highlands police log entries for February 12, 1931. *Muriel J. Smith.*

to the hospital, which I did. The man was a soldier, so I took him to hospital at Sandy Hook. The doctor claimed it was either bad liquor or appendicitis."

George Hardy was the mayor of Highlands and played a leading role with the police department, with police logs showing numerous times when he was called to a situation, called the police himself or simply assisted with a need.

Take Patrol Officer Johnson's report of September 7, 1930, for instance. He must have either completed his log at the end of his duty that day or simply forgot to include one occurrence when it happened, since he put a 3:45 p.m. incident before the record of a 3:30 incident. The official report reads: "At 3:45, Paul J. Bartck of Fort Hancock, NJ was driving a car with a permit but no driver's license. And caused an accident by hitting a car on Bay Ave in front of Straus's Restaurant. The car that car hit was driven by Edward F. Halligan, 37 2nd St, Rumson, driver's license No. 36021. Reg. No 10198 owned by James F. Halligan. Reg. No of car driven by Paul J. Bartck Reg No 12523 owned by Fred W. Shrerich Fort Hancock."

There is no report about whether there were injuries, summons issued, tests taken for sobriety or any other action—until after the next report. That entry reads: "At 3:30 p.m. was called to Franklin's Restaurant as Franklin dropped dead in yard back of restaurant. The local doctors were not in town. Mayor Hardy got Dr. C. Woodruff of Atlantic Highlands." That's all the report says about poor Mr. Franklin. But Officer Johnson continued: "While Dr. Woodruff was here, he examined Paul Bartck. He did not find him sufficiently under the influence of liquids as to be unfit to drive a car."

On another date, Patrol Officer Lawrence wrote that at 3:30 a.m., a man "came to the door of the court room nude. I questioned him as to what was the matter, but could not get him to talk, so I coaxed him into a cell. He got violent, so I called Mayor Hardy and by his order I called Dr. Rowland. Doctor gave me some pills to give him, but he would not take them. He bumped his head on cell and cut same. Doctor came, dressed wound and gave him a shot to quiet him so officers could take him to Freehold.… Got coffee and buns and sandwich for him and another prisoner." Officer Johnson added the man "was committed to Freehold by Mayor Hardy for disorderly conduct and dangerously insane. I notified [the man's wife] that he was to be sent to Freehold, and Officer Monahan went with Joe Andrews to Freehold with prisoner." There is no mention of whether the gentleman was clothed or unclothed en route to the county jail.

Officer Monahan's reports are equally devoid of details but just as fascinating to read in the twenty-first century. His report shows that even in the 1930s, residents called police for any number of reasons, including to collect rent.

On February 12, 1931, Officer Monahan, who was on duty from 10:30 p.m. to 9:00 a.m., listed his routine duties of general patrol, door and light inspections and a half hour of directing school traffic beginning at 8:30 a.m., then wrote: "At 11 p.m. was called to Mrs. Dempsey on Bay Avenue and Cedar St. about a fellow who was going to leave town and owed her two dollars for a room. He said he had no money but would send it to her. His name is Sergeant Erkman of US Marine Corps, Lakehurst, NJ. No arrest made." One wonders whether Sergeant Erkman ever sent the two dollars.

During one of his door checks, Officer Monahan noted that the door was open at the Highlands Garage, but when he notified Frank Weinheimer, the owner of the garage, about it, he was told "it was alright."

Patrol Officer Kyril Parker's log showed the cooperation police enjoyed with telephone operators—the ladies who manned the switchboards and connected two parties who wanted to talk to each other on the phone.

One summer's night, while Parker was on duty from 8:00 p.m. to 6:00 a.m., he received a call at 3:00 a.m. from a man on Navesink Avenue. The log notes that he "would not give his name, but we got it from the operator that it was George Schmidt that called. Was in regard of some noise there. Officer Rubley took me there and we found some fellows having a party. We told them to stop it and they did so."

There was no shortage of calls relating to Prohibition, with more than a few of them at Conner's Hotel, always a popular restaurant and bar—and operated at that time by the first generation of the family business, husband and wife William and Mary Conners. Conner's Hotel was later run by the Conners's daughter and her husband, Marie and Herman Black, then by their sons, the brothers Black (William, Herman, John and Robert). In most cases, no action was taken, and police never found anything wrong.

In August 1930, Patrol Officer Johnson reported that "county men raided Tom and Mark Anthony's place on Waterwitch Ave. I was with them while they raided. They got a large still." A couple of days later, Johnson reported that he received a call from the prosecutor's office to notify the Anthonys "to be in Freehold this afternoon without fail. They were notified at 11:45 a.m. I notified Tom Mark Antony's wife to tell her husband for he was out of town. I notified Joe Mark Antony personally."

It was the Depression, Prohibition and a less sophisticated time. And it was fun.

—From the *Atlantic Highlands Herald*, January 11, 2018

14

THE REAL McCOY

By Muriel J. Smith

Andrew J. Volstead was a well-known but very unpopular name in the years following World War I. A congressman from Minnesota, Volstead was the author of the Volstead Act, the first step in the struggle to enforce the Eighteenth Amendment to the Constitution—the amendment that tried to ban the sale of intoxicating liquors to every person in the nation.

But Volstead—and most members of Congress who approved the act in January 1919 and put Prohibition in place—also gave rise to new words, new names and new heroes, especially along the Monmouth County Bayshore.

Bootlegging, rumrunning and speakeasies all became part of the American vernacular. Bootleggers, originally named for the men who hid flasks of alcohol in their boot tops while trading with Native Americans in the West during the 1880s, became those who dealt in illicit liquids in the 1920s; speakeasies, sometimes called "blind pigs" or "blind tigers," were the "Speak Softly Shops" where those illicit liquids could be purchased and about which one spoke in soft tones. A "burlock" was a case that contained a half-dozen bottles of liquor stacked two-high, with each wrapped in straw, then sewn into a burlap bag. These were also known as "sacks" (by the Coast Guard) or "hams" (by the rumrunners).

In the later years of Prohibition, the lucrative business was completely dominated by organized crime, but in the early days, it was basically hardworking fishermen, clammers, boat owners and boatbuilders who took advantage of an exciting way to make a living.

Along Monmouth County's waterways, during the early years of the "Social Experiment," the name that was revered and the man with whom to do business was William F. "Bill" McCoy.

The son of a Civil War navy veteran, Bill McCoy was born in Syracuse, New York, in 1877 and raised in Florida after his family moved there seven years after his birth. He was a hardworking and adventurous waterman whose father had instilled in him a love for the sea. He graduated first in his class from a Pennsylvania cadet training school and mated for twenty years on steamships in the Caribbean before heading back to Florida to partner with his brother Ben in a boatbuilding business. The brothers were known for their honesty, dependability and expertise with building sturdy, safe boats.

It was just this talent that brought an acquaintance to the shipyard one day who explained the income possible simply by captaining a boat filled with liquor from the islands to the coast off of New Jersey. Although Bill turned down that original offer, primarily because he did not think the schooner offered for the work was seaworthy enough, he was enticed by the idea and decided to find his own boat and start the business himself.

The brothers sold the boats in their shipyard, and the ninety-foot schooner *Henry L. Marshall* became the vessel for Bill McCoy's return to the ocean as a sea captain. Successful from the start, McCoy soon went for a bigger, faster boat; it wasn't long before the *Arethusa* began making frequent trips between the Bahamas and the three miles off the Jersey coast from Atlantic City to Perth Amboy. The ship sailed under a new name, the *Tomoka*, and was registered in Great Britain. But to Bill, it would always be the *Arethusa*.

Bill McCoy, honest, hardworking and dependable as he was, also knew in the early days of Prohibition that there were few revenue cutters pursuing smugglers, and of them, most could be outrun if a pursuit was underway. However, he was careful to keep his craft in the safety of international waters, never venturing closer to New Jersey's shores than three miles off the shore. It was there that McCoy, the newly arrived smuggler, would rendezvous with the boats of the men who clammed and fished by day and met the *Tomoka* by night to bring supplies to a thirsty public.

When others followed McCoy's habits of staying somewhat close to shore but still in international waters, Rum Row was founded; Rum Row was the long stream of large vessels laden with rum, scotch, whiskey and other spirits that awaited the transfer to eager purchasers, who would then carry cases, bags and bottles the rest of the way to shore. The burlocks, which made the transition and portage easier and accommodated the least space, were a McCoy creation.

It was his honesty that once again made Bill McCoy the most popular and eagerly sought-after rumrunner. As competition increased, captains became greedier, and buyers remained unaware. Many diluted their island purchases to increase their sales of more bottles, barrels and cases—but not Bill McCoy. He was in the business for the money, but not at the cost of cheating his customers. It wasn't long before word got around, and a sales pitch became known on land: if you got your liquor from the *Tomoka*, it was the real, unadulterated thing…the real McCoy.

In 1923, McCoy's *Tomoka* was engaged in a battle with Coast Guardsmen who boarded the ship in international waters. When he continued to flee with the revenuers still aboard, and his ship was fired upon, he gave up and was eventually brought up on charges in Middlesex County for violations of the Volstead Act.

McCoy spent eight months in jail for rumrunning—a time that was not entirely uncomfortable because of the camaraderie between some wealthy smugglers and the prison staff. By the time McCoy was again a free man, organized crime had taken over the bootlegging business. So, McCoy walked away from a trade that had been lucrative, outside the law and adventurous, although he was never harmful or dishonest to his customers.

When it ceased to be fun, Bill McCoy—the real McCoy—returned to Florida, where he invested in real estate and never worked again. He died on December 30, 1948, of a heart attack and is buried in Stuart, Florida.

—From the *Atlantic Highlands Herald*, April 14, 2014

PART II: OLD SHREWSBURY

15

CHRIST CHURCH IN SHREWSBURY

By Rick Geffken

"I give and bequeath my houses and lands and plantations and all my real estate in Middletown and County of Monmouth and Province of New Jersey, after the death of my wife and helpless brother, to the venerable and honorable Society for the Propagation of the Gospel in Foreign Parts, and to their successors forever, to and for the use and purpose following; that is to say, for the use and purpose of a perpetual glebe for the use and habitation of a Minister of the said Society to preach the Gospel to the inhabitants of Middletown and Shrewsbury."
—Will of William Leeds Jr., June 20, 1735

William Leeds Sr. was born in 1650, before his family migrated from Essex, England, to East Jersey. His parents, Thomas and Mary Leeds, were the founders of the colonial branch of the family; Thomas Leeds was fifty-seven when he arrived at Little Silver Point in Shrewsbury, Monmouth County. He and Mary obtained warrants for 240 acres of land from the East Jersey Proprietors. Mary died shortly afterward, but their three sons survived. William was the eldest.

When he was not quite twenty years old, William married Dorothea Scilton (possibly Tilton), who was seventeen years old. They, too, were granted a warrant—this one for 120 acres of Middletown land. William was a cooper (barrel-maker) by trade. He was successful enough to accumulate other tracts of land. Significantly, he bought tracts north of the Swimming River from Richard Stout. The second deed, from 1679, described the purchase:

Richard Stoutt [sic] and Francis [sic] his wife of Midletown in the County of Naborsinks in the province of new Jersey, the one party, and William Leeds of Shroofberry within the county and province aforesaid, the other party, witness that the said Richard Stoutt and Francis his wife have cleavely bargained and sold, and by these presents cleavely bargained and selleth, for the said William Leeds, the mannour of land with the appurtenances that lyeth by the Swiming ribor within the bounds of Midletowne with all the buildings, fences, outyards, and meadows, both fresh meadows and boggy meadows, and upland as well as cleared land, and uncleared land and all the wood and underwood with all and singular their appurtenances, and all mannour of gains, profits, and advantages arysering upon the land.

Five years later, in partnership with Daniel Applegate, Leeds purchased more land from local Lenape Indians. One of these deeds reads:

From Iraseek, Sachem of Wickaton, to William Leeds and Daniel Applegate, conveys a tract of land in Middletown or Chawcosett, called by the name of Climes Kake, which tract was marked out by Seahoppra, an uncle of Iraseek, in the presence of his brother, Necktoha and Powraas: consideration of the deed is four yards of Duffels, or equivalent in Rum, to be paid each year on the first of November, for three hundred and fifteen years from date, to Iraseek, his heirs or assign.

Applegate and Leeds soon had adjoining farms in the area known as Leedsville (today's Lincroft). The small settlement was at the junction of the roads between Tinton Falls and Middletown. A tavern opened there as early as 1717 to accommodate travelers.

In 1694, William Leeds decided to move to West Jersey and gave 184 acres of his land to his son, William Leeds Jr.:

The care of the farm and of his mother and helpless brother and possibly of his sister Mary devolved upon William Leeds, the second, the grandson of Thomas, the emigrant. His mother was named Dorothea. It was not until after the death of his mother and of his imbecile brother, that William Leeds, the second, late in life, married Rebecca (sometimes, Rebekah), the daughter of Peter and Rebecca Tilton, and the widow of his one-time neighbor, Daniel Applegate.

The combined Leeds/Applegate property now comprised well over four hundred acres of rich farmland along Hop Brook, upon which was a splendid house. The house was undoubtedly that built by William Sr. in 1687.

The Leeds home and furnishings were apparently so much grander than those of their neighbors that many speculated about the source of his income. Rumors circulated that Leeds had been an associate of a contemporary New York seaman, Captain William Kidd. Originally a privateer, Kidd is more infamous as a pirate whose "treasure" was never found. Some thought Leeds knew of its location and used it to furnish his lavish lifestyle. The legend concerning Leeds may have resulted from a crewmember of Kidd's with a similar name. Contrary to the pirate myth, which has been debunked, William Leeds Jr. was an ardent churchgoer.

William Jr. and Rebekah Leeds, both in their late forties when they married, had no children. They apparently thought for some time about donating their land to Christ Church. A 1732 letter from Reverend William Skinner of Perth Amboy states:

> *A donation hath actually been made about the month of August last of a farm of 200 acres of well improved land with a good house, out houses, barn and orchard on the Premises at a small distance from the Church with the reserve only of the lives of two old people, a man and his wife. Upon this, the Society have appointed the Reverend Mr. John Forbes, Missionary there.*

Thus, Reverend Forbes became the first of the ministers of Christ Church to live on the old farm, which was designated as a glebe.

William Leeds's 1735 will provided for Rebekah to continue to live on the Leedsville farm until her passing. In it, he requested that his body be buried by the body of his mother. He gave five pounds to his brother Thomas, and the rest of his estate went to Rebekah, including the care of his helpless brother Daniel. Upon the deaths of Rebekah and Daniel, his moveable estate was bequeathed to others, but his lands went to Christ Church. William Leeds Jr. died on April 29, 1739, and was laid to rest near his home, close to the Hop Brook branch of the Swimming River. In 1906, his remains were removed and reinterred beneath a stone near the entrance to Christ Church Shrewsbury.

For the next one hundred years, Christ Church used the 438-acre gift as a working farm, or glebe, for its ministers. It provided them with supplemental income as their congregations became established. Christ

Christ Church Shrewsbury was completed in 1769 due to the efforts of Reverend Samuel Cooke. *McKay Imaging Photography.*

Church stated: "A large and fertile farm was no inconsiderable addition for the yearly allowance of £60 from the Society for the Propagation of the Gospel in Foreign Parts (SPG)."

Christ Church is recognized as being organized on December 25, 1702, in the Tintern Manor home of Lewis Morris in Shrewsbury Township. On that date, Reverend George Keith, missionary of the SPG, preached to Lewis and Isabella Morris and probably William Leeds, the Reverend Alexander Innes and others. In 1706, Nicholas Brown gave property to the SPG for the building of a permanent church. The land was on the southeast of what became known as the Four Corners along the Main Road to Eatontown and the road to Tinton Falls. However, it would take some years before a permanent structure was built sometime between 1715 and 1733, when Reverend John Forbes began his ministry there. That first building was described as "of brick and lime…the best proportioned structure in the county." It was about thirty feet by twenty-four feet and fronted north along the Tinton Falls to Shrewsbury Road (today's Sycamore Avenue).

The glebe farm is referred to in many subsequent church documents and records. The earliest mention is in December 1752: "It is agreed that Mr. Josiah Halstead, Mr. James Russell, Mr. Thorn and Mr. Redford do take a view of the house upon the glebe and make a report to the next meeting of the vestry what repairs and additions it requires and what sum will be sufficient for making those repairs and additions in a handsome

This cenotaph was erected to honor the memory of William Leeds Jr. at Christ Church Episcopal Church in Middletown in 1906. *Library of Congress.*

manner." Since this was soon after the appointment of Reverend Samuel Cooke, the seventy-five-year-old house must have needed updating before it was suitable for him.

Reverend Cooke and his wife, Graham (née Kearney), lived on the glebe for a time after their 1756 marriage. Cooke started selling subscriptions for the construction of a new church building, which was completed in 1769. Life became more difficult for Cooke in the years following the loss of his wife during childbirth in 1771. An outspoken Loyalist, he fled to England in 1775. His personal property was confiscated during the Revolutionary War, and a Christ Church vestryman, Josiah Holmes, took the glebe for himself.

Although having a layperson live on the glebe may seem contradictory to William Leeds's intentions, there are at least two reasons Holmes may have felt justified in his action. First, Christ Church had no missionary during the years of the Revolution, so the glebe would have remained empty and neglected. Second, Leeds's will had stipulated:

> *And whereas, it may so happen that the Minister, Missionary, or Rector into whose hands and possession my said house, lands, and estate may come, may commit great waste on the same, rendering it thereby of less value to his successors, or may be guilty of immoralities to the scandal of religion and of his profession, it is my will that my executors…may expel such Minister, Missionary, or Rector so commiting [sic] waste or being guilty of immoralities…from my said house and lands, and shall hire the same…for the benefit of the next Minister, and so from time to time, as often as such case shall happen.*

So, putting aside whether loyalty to the king is scandalous or immoral, it appears that Holmes had a convincing argument for the other vestrymen that he had the right to take the glebe. Holmes could have persuaded his fellows that he would be an interim caretaker until a new minister could be appointed. That did not happen until Henry Wardell was appointed in 1788. We don't know how long Holmes stayed in the glebe, but he died in 1789.

The glebe continued to be used by church ministers for another sixty years or so. In 1854, Christ Church split into two congregations—the original in Shrewsbury and one in Middletown. In 1854, the New Jersey State Legislature passed a law with two significant provisions. First, it incorporated each congregation as being "the said minister, church wardens, and vestry." This gave formal title to these American branches of the SPG, superseding the 1738 Crown charter. Second, the law allowed for a division of the glebe between the two new church entities. The Shrewsbury congregation was granted the eastern and slightly larger section—250 acres of the 438-acre total.

In March 1888, Christ Church of Middletown sold its portion of the former glebe to David D. Withers, a nationally prominent horseman. He had partnered with several other well-heeled men to purchase Monmouth Racetrack in 1878. Withers converted the glebe to a large racehorse farm, which he called Brookdale Farm, that spanned both sides of Newman Springs Road.

The construction of a parsonage next to the Shrewsbury Church in 1824–25 basically ended the glebe's use as a full-time ministerial residence. It remained a source for firewood and probably provided some produce for ministers and their families. Eventually, the Shrewsbury church sold off its half of the glebe in two separate transactions. In 1900, the Tinton Manor Water Company purchased 75 acres along the Swimming River. Reverend William Bailey signed the deed. The water company built a dam just west of the Tinton Falls–Lincroft Road, and the resulting reservoir provided water for Middletown and the surrounding area.

In 1906, the last 175 acres of the original Shrewsbury glebe were sold to Joseph Raab. In November, church wardens decided to move the remains of William Leeds Jr. to the Christ Church Cemetery in Shrewsbury. His remains were found to be in good condition, indicating that William Leeds Jr. was a tall, well-built man. He was reburied under a stone just to the left of the church entrance. A cenotaph commemorating William Leeds Jr. was erected in the Christ Church Middletown Cemetery on Kings Highway.

The Lincroft School, Thompson Park, the campus of Brookdale Community College and the American Water Company all occupy the old glebe property today.

—From the *Crown* (newsletter of Christ Church Shrewsbury), December 2013

16

OLD GRAVEYARD YIELDS
NEW DISCOVERIES

By Rick Geffken

To a casual observer, the old grave markers in Christ Church Cemetery in Shrewsbury all look about the same, featuring old-style lettering, simple engravings and the dates and ages of the deceased. But on the evening of Thursday, January 7, 2016, Monmouth University senior Taylor Cavanaugh presented the Shrewsbury Historical Society with a more nuanced view.

"There were actually three distinct periods of iconography on the stones," she told the audience of over forty people. "Mortality imagery; cherubs; and, finally, neoclassical carvings each appear in defined clusters."

A history and archaeology major, Cavanaugh had just completed her senior thesis after spending months studying the numerous graves in the famed Episcopal churchyard at Broad Street and Sycamore Avenue in Shrewsbury. The young scholar spoke about her findings at the society's headquarters and museum building just across the street from Christ Church. Both buildings are part of the historic "Four Corners."

In the fall of 2015, Cavanaugh worked as an intern under the auspices of Christ Church historian Robert M. Kelly Jr. She studied, photographed and analyzed about fifty individual headstones. She found a surprising consistency of styles within specific timeframes.

"The earliest and simplest grave markers in the church yard date to the seventeenth century," Cavanaugh observed. "Many of these stones have hourglass or death-head (skull) imagery. These primitive mortality images were used to remind the living of their eventual fate." This style almost certainly originated in New England and was brought south to Monmouth County by settlers from the Rhode Island Colony. In fact, the stones themselves were probably quarried in Rhode Island, then transported by ship to New Jersey.

By the 1720s or 1730s, the first noticeable shift in imagery occurred, likely connected to the First Great Awakening religious revival in America. Grave markers from this period were illustrated with tiny winged cherubs. These depictions, Cavanaugh noted, indicate that "people were developing a more spiritual outlook, one that emphasized the soul's flight from earth to heaven." The stones sometimes featured acanthus-leaf carvings along their borders. These filigrees reflected the newfound tastes of the East Jersey colony's emerging middle class. It was evolving to become a consumer culture with more disposable income.

The Shrewsbury community, largely agricultural in its early days, added specialty occupations like blacksmiths, woodworkers, and stonecutters in the mid- to late eighteenth century. These small businesses generated wealth for their owners. Increased earnings and savings allowed people to buy more expensive day-to-day items, such as matched dishware and cutlery sets and, of course, gravestones with more artistic carvings.

The second shift in gravestone imagery occurred after the Revolutionary War and was concurrent with the spread of new Protestant denominations. Cavanaugh documented a pattern of more elaborate grave marker carvings. Families who had made it to the top of society, like the Stelles in Shrewsbury, began to commission stone carvers to commemorate their deceased loved ones with fashion in mind. The memorials began to change from rococo (ornate, curving styles) to neoclassical ornamentation. Willow trees, urns, and monograms appeared. There was even some competitiveness, as well-to-do families showed off their status by erecting taller headstones than their poorer contemporaries.

Cavanaugh's research illustrates how headstones accurately mirrored the cultural changes in early New Jersey history. She graduated from Monmouth University and, as of 2019, was continuing her studies there in pursuit of a master's degree in anthropology.

—From the *Two River Times*, June 9, 2016

17

HISTORIC PARKER HOMESTEAD IN LITTLE SILVER

By Rick Geffken

Agroup that operates Little Silver's historic Parker House was recently awarded two preservation grants. The nonprofit Parker Homestead - 1665, Inc., will use the grants to further its mission to restore and operate the historic homestead and grounds located at 235 Rumson Road in Little Silver. President and trustee Keith Wells expressed delight when he was notified of the awards: "These generous matching grants will help us continue to be a more active, modern organization and a true community resource."

As the name of the nonprofit indicates, the Parker House was built in 1665 and was one of the earliest permanent farm residences in Monmouth County. Wells believes it may be the oldest homestead continually occupied by one family in the entire United States—Parker descendants lived, farmed and flourished there for over 330 years. The last person to live in the home was eighth-generation family member Julia Parker, who died without heirs in 1995. Her will deeded the remaining ten acres of her family's historic land, her home and the outbuildings to the Borough of Little Silver.

The late trustee Liz Hanson liked to say:

> Name an event in American history up to 1995. The Parkers were living in this house when it happened, not necessarily directly involved but knowing and talking about it and experiencing the times around these events. The Parkers were active drivers in shaping what Little Silver has become.

Physically, through their land donations; spiritually, with their strong (but evolving) religious beliefs; and politically, for their financial support for the institutions they made happen.

In January, Parker Homestead - 1665, Inc., was notified of a $3,000 matching grant, called a GOS (General Operating Support) grant, from the State of New Jersey. The organization is obligated to match it with its own funds used to offset ongoing utility and insurance bills, as well as programming events such as last year's re-creation of an 1864 baseball game held on the field in front of the house.

The second grant came in February from the Monmouth County Historical Commission. It was another matching grant, one for $4,700, which will be used to restore a sweet potato frame directly behind the Parker House. Consulting original building plans and pictures, Wells found the frame was in active use until about twenty years ago. He personally cleared brush and pumped groundwater from the deteriorated wooden greenhouse constructed on top of a concrete foundation.

"As we researched what we had here," Wells says, "We discovered this sweet potato frame was unique in New Jersey. Our contractor will soon start to rebuild it, using the original wood components as templates, and

Shown here around 1900, young Doug Parker was among the last of eight generations of his family who lived in this home. *The Parker Homestead - 1665, Inc.*

the salvaged glass windows. We're considering using it as part of the on-site community garden." The rebuild was completed in time for the May 2019 Weekend in Old Monmouth, an annual event sponsored by the Monmouth County Board of Chosen Freeholders and the Monmouth County Historical Commission.

Wells went on to explain that the sweet potatoes were not actually grown to harvest in the frame. The Parkers would plant thousands of "slips," or young sweet potato plants, in the interior soil during late winter and early spring. An attached heater, improvised from spare farm machinery parts, pumped hot water to keep the plants alive through colder days and nights. Wells smiled when he said: "The Parkers never wasted a thing. Old equipment was repurposed continually. We have a barn load full of old metal farming equipment." Once the slips were established, the Parkers sold them to other farmers for replanting.

Melissa Ziobro, another trustee, who teaches at Monmouth University, is particularly excited about the symbiotic relationship that has developed between the Parker Homestead and the university. She notes: "The Homestead has really become a learning laboratory for students interested in history and archaeology as they participate in digs."

The Parker Homestead - 1665, Inc., is run by a volunteer board, consisting of four trustees, which manages the Parker home, barns and four and a half acres of land, which is leased from the borough. Little Silver mayor Bob Neff Jr. commented: "The Parker Homestead is a beautiful site, sitting on top of that rolling hill. It doesn't just benefit the borough, but also the whole state. It has tremendous cultural, historic, academic, and aesthetic import." Neff is happy to point out that "the Parker Homestead foundation raises funds through grants and events, taking the burden from the Little Silver taxpayers."

A full slate of events can be seen at www.parkerhomestead-1665.org. Volunteers needed for any of the dozens of opportunities can call Keith Wells at (908) 489-2503 or email him at keithbwells@gmail.com. He emphasizes: "We don't want to be a museum but rather a community resource with an historical foundation."

—From the *Two River Times*, March 22–29, 2018

18

Students Dig
Little Silver History

By Rick Geffken

Archaeology students from Monmouth University were just as thrilled to find the bits of glass, shells and animal bones they unearthed at the historic Parker Homestead as they were to find the pipe stem, pottery shards and the 1887 coin. Taken together, these finds from a preliminary dig at the Little Silver landmark are intriguing clues to the day-to-day living patterns and Quaker culture of the Parker family, who lived and farmed here for over 330 years.

Working under the direction of Monmouth University (MU) archaeologist Dr. Richard Veit on Friday, March 30, 2018, graduate students uncovered these seemingly innocuous leftovers just a few inches down in a small patch of grass directly behind the Parker Homestead (sometimes referred to as the Parker House). Dr. Veit, chair of the history and archaeology department at MU, has long considered the Parker Homestead particularly interesting.

"It's a place with a well-documented history back to the initial settlements of New Jersey," Veit says. "The Parker House's proximity to Monmouth University and its active Friends organization make this almost a Monmouth University field station. My students are able to contribute to the presentation and interpretation of a very important historical site in our own community."

One of the budding archaeologists getting her hands dirty last Friday was Jamie Esposito of Middletown. The enthusiastic young woman will be earning credits toward her master of anthropology degree while she interns at the Parker House this summer.

"I hope to use this intern experience to make artifact displays at the Parker House interesting for all age groups. This will help me reach my goal of working in biological archaeology and osteology." She explains those technical terms as meaning "forensic analysis working with bones."

Other local students at the dig included Katie Serkus of Union Beach and Peter Samaras of Middletown. They took turns using a sifter to look for artifacts. The device is basically a screen mounted on a moveable frame. Shovelfuls of dirt are placed on the screen and shaken back and forth until the dirt drops through onto a tarp, and, with luck, small objects are left atop the screen. They are put in plastic bags with notes describing where they were found for later analysis. At the conclusion of the dig, the sifted dirt is placed back in the holes, and the turf plug is replaced.

The Parker House dig was postponed for a week due to our last snowy nor'easter. Before beginning the dig on the overcast, early spring morning, Veit took his students through the old home for an introduction to its construction and history. He explained to them how the house was built in phases over several hundred years, pointing to the varying styles of beams, flooring, clay and horsehair insulation and brickwork.

Marilyn Scherfen of Atlantic Highlands is happy to be working alongside students somewhat younger than she is (a journalist did not inquire). After retiring in 2012 from her longtime position as Atlantic Highlands librarian, she "took a part time job, but managed to spend a few days at Dr. Veit's Sandy Hook Lighthouse dig two summers ago. One day, my hand came across something that looked like a pebble, but it was too heavy. I thought 'It's lead, a musket ball.' From then on, I was enchanted and told myself I wanted to do more of this. I made an appointment with Dr. Veit at MU and asked him if it made sense at my age to get involved in this. He's such a charismatic person, he draws people in. I'm now enrolled in the master's program for anthropology. I honestly don't know where this will lead, but my 'personal history' will be made later."

One intriguing aspect of the Parker family history is the question of slavery. A family legend about a long wooden bench in the house's cellar says it was where "servants" ate. Keith Wells, president of the nonprofit Parker Homestead - 1665, Inc., continues to research this fraught topic and has found evidence that early Parkers did indeed own slaves. "An intern researched Parker family wills and last testaments a while ago, and slaves are mentioned a few times. As distasteful and shocking as this may be to us today, in the eighteenth and nineteenth centuries, some Monmouth County family farms used slaves. We'll be looking at ways to present this unpleasant truth with sensitivity as we tell the story of this place."

Wells concluded, "This dig is important because we have a really great relationship with MU, particularly Dr. Veit and Professor of History Melissa Ziobro. The ultimate find would be the foundation or evidence of the first house on the property. The current structure dating from 1721 was built over the original put up in the mid-1660s. We believe the fireplace and chimney, with its beehive oven space, were part of the first house."

—From the *Two River Times*, May 10–17, 2018

19

Love and Marriage: European Royalty and American Women

By Rick Geffken

Though much of the hoopla surrounding the marriage of Prince Harry and Meghan Markle has mercifully passed, Monmouth University professor Melissa Ziobro reminded a Tinton Falls audience that the recent British matrimonial event was just the latest in a tradition of across-the-pond "romances" between members of the European royalty and American brides.

On Monday, May 21, Professor Ziobro regaled twenty-five very interested senior women (and two brave men) with stories of "American Women and Royal Marriages." The Harry/Meghan wedding was certainly spectacular, with the young lovers arriving at their nuptials in an open-topped Ascot Landau carriage pulled by Windsor Grey horses from the Royal Mews, but the joining together of Old and New World couples was not as uncommon as we might think.

Ziobro is a specialist professor of public history in the Department of History and Anthropology at Monmouth University and frequently writes and lectures on women's issues. During this recent presentation, Ziobro admitted that "there are important issues and there are interesting issues. This most recent royal wedding falls into the latter, but it has increased attention to the Gilded Age phenomena of what were called 'American Dollar Princesses.' By some counts, there may have been as many as five hundred of these marriages between American women of 'new money' who were betrothed to the relatively impoverished European aristocracy." Their motivations included trading "cash for class." How's that? Well, after the American Civil War, an explosion of the number of U.S. millionaires provided the opportunity. Many of the daughters of the newly wealthy saw titled European nobility as a way to attain duchess—or even princess—status.

In Europe, the Industrial Revolution had drained landholders of tenant farmers, who were fleeing to the cities for new factory jobs. The landed gentry

Florence Hazard of Shrewsbury was only sixteen years old when she married Prince Franz von Auersperg of Austria in June 1899. *Library of Congress.*

needed to find income to replace their disappearing earnings from centuries-old agricultural endeavors. Their expensive-to-maintain manor houses were becoming increasingly unsustainable, as well. Enter American money. Although British nobility became the top choice for most young women seeking these marriages, they also married Germans, Austrians and Italians.

Sixty-plus years before Meghan Markle walked, starry-eyed, down the aisle of St. George's Chapel to wed Prince Harry in Windsor Castle, older Americans still remember when movie star Grace Kelly married Prince Rainier III of Monaco in 1956. Both appear to be true-love matches, not exchanges of hard currency for titles—Harry does not lack for resources.

Ziobro noted that the television series *Downton Abbey* sparked her to examine the unusual arranged marriages between American women and English titled gentlemen, which began in the late nineteenth century. She laughed recalling how the subject caught her attention: "I was watching *Downton Abbey*, and like any good historian, I can't watch TV and enjoy myself; I have to start researching things, like who Cora Crawley, Countess of Grantham, was modeled after." Ziobro soon discovered that some New Jersey women were among the many "American Dollar Princesses."

American newspapers often ran lists of American heiresses marrying noblemen, including the amount of money the young women "took out of the country" with them—often $500,000 or more. Of particular interest to *Two River Times* readers, and probably surprising to most, is the story of Florence Hazard of Shrewsbury, daughter of E.C. Hazard, the owner of the world-famous Hazard Ketchup Factory. Florence was only sixteen years old when she married Prince Franz von Auersperg of Austria in June 1899 at Shrewsbury. She was looking to improve her station in life—and, incidentally, her fiancé's.

Von Auersperg was part of a noble family and had enjoyed a spirited (which is to say wanton) youth, according to contemporary accounts at the time of the wedding. One paper noted: "The engagement is hailed by court and aristocratic circles with gratification, as the Prince seemed to have hopelessly wrecked his life by fast living and gambling before he left Vienna three years ago." Though he was studying to be a physician in Long Island when he met Florence Hazard, her father's success no doubt made her more attractive to von Auersperg. After years of creditors chasing down the von Auerspergs, Florence finally had enough and divorced the prince in 1915.

—From the *Two River Times*, June 7, 2018

20

Old Shrewsbury Township Map Discovered and Interpreted

By Rick Geffken

A few years ago, Don and Mary Lea Burden, president and treasurer, respectively, of the Shrewsbury Historical Society (SHS), were sorting through the hundreds of documents and artifacts in the society's museum. Most everything there was collected and assembled by the late J. Louise Jost, who apparently never missed a print mention of Shrewsbury.

After searching through a dusty museum closet, the Burdens unrolled a fragile, old 1849 map of Shrewsbury Township. The hand-drawn map depicts houses, churches and waterways in the township almost seventy-five years before the incorporation of the current borough. The initials "BWC" below the scale indicator ("30 chains to the inch") were likely those of the surveyor who drew it.

Why was the now-crumbling chart drawn, and who was "BWC?" Is it important, and should it be preserved? SHS member Rick Geffken and Don Burden took the map to the offices of the Monmouth County archivist Gary Saretzky in Manalapan for his advice. Saretzky suggested the map was indeed unique and recommended that the famed Conservation Center for Art & Historic Artifacts in Philadelphia was the best place to bring it for preservation before it completely turned to dust.

Perhaps the map had something to do with the creation of Ocean County in 1850, when that large section of real estate was lopped off of southern Monmouth County. Or, possibly, it was created to outline new boundaries when Ocean Township was separated from Shrewsbury in 1849. The initials "BWC" might be an important clue to either possibility.

Rick Geffken (*left*) and Don Burden examine a deteriorated 1849 map with a conservator at the Conservation Center for Art & Historic Artifacts in Philadelphia. *Rick Geffken.*

Don Burden and Geffken made the trip to the Conservation Center for Art & Historic Artifacts in February 2018 to drop off the map for evaluation. A few weeks later, paper conservator Heather Hendry provided the SHS with conservation costs in the $5,000–$8,000 range. The actual project of map conservation and research into its contextual history may take a year—a relatively short time compared to the 169 years since the map's creation. SHS president Don Burden says the SHS will apply for grant money and eventually hopes to sell full-sized reproductions to offset some of these costs.

The map encompasses an area from the Navesink River at its top (northern part) to the Shark River at its bottom (southern part). The western boundaries are Freehold and Howell; the eastern boundary is the Atlantic Ocean. The inscriptions on "A Map of the Township of Shrewsbury" indicate that it was drawn in "January 1849" by someone with the initials "BWC." Black ink was used for town names, buildings, streams, and so forth. Pencil notations of dotted "present line" and "proposed line" are evident between Shrewsbury Town (centered on the Four Corners) and Eatontown (incorporated in 1873). These are strong indicators that it was created to show demarcations between these municipalities.

The Township of Ocean was created by an act of the New Jersey legislature on February 21, 1849, from portions of Shrewsbury Township, at which time the newly formed township stretched from the Shrewsbury River to the southern tip of Avon-by-the-Sea. This comports with the scope of the map.

The top of the map is rolled onto a black-painted dowel, attached by brads, and its bottom is attached to a black, L-shaped piece of what looks like corner molding. Thus, the map was likely used for presentations to public audiences—possibly to the New Jersey legislature itself—to illustrate the proposed separation of Shrewsbury and Ocean Township.

According to the Township of Ocean League of Women Voters:

> *By the middle of the nineteenth century, eastern Monmouth County had outgrown its single township government. The burgeoning populations and developing businesses of the lands incorporated into Shrewsbury a century and a half before required government more responsive to local needs. It included all lands from Sea Bright south to the Shark River and west to encompass Eatontown and Neptune. Growth and development continued. Communities within the incorporated boundaries of the Township of Ocean themselves began to require more parochial representation.*

The Monmouth County Historical Association, headquartered at 70 Court Street in Freehold, was incorporated in 1898 to "discover, procure, preserve and perpetuate whatever relates to the history of Monmouth County." Its museum collections include many old maps, one of which is a "traced copy" of the 1849 map under examination. Two inscriptions on the tracing attribute the map to two different surveyors: Britton W. Corlies (in 1843) and Benjamin W. Corlies (in 1849). The latter inscription appears older and possibly is contemporary with the map's creation.

Britton W. Corlies (1789–1840) and Benjamin W. Corlies (1797–1884) were brothers, the sons of Britton Corlies and Sara Woolley. But Britton W. Corlies (Jr.) died in July 1840, nine years before the creation of the map and three years before the inscription next to his name, so that inscription must be a mistake. Can we prove that Benjamin Woolley Corlies drew the map?

Benjamin W. Corlies inherited Eatontown property as per his father's will of April 17, 1811 (Britton Corlies Sr. died in October 1816). The Monmouth

County Archives has several maps and references confirming B.W. Corlies living in Eatontown: the Lightfoot map of 1851 and the F.W. Beers map of 1873, as well as Corlies family information in several genealogy records.

Benjamin W. Corlies is mentioned in numerous Monmouth County documents during his lifetime. For example, he was appointed trustee of his cousin George Corlies's (1749–1817) estate in 1837; in 1846, he was appointed guardian of his cousin Edward Pennington Corlies. He was elected one of the vice presidents of the Monmouth County Agricultural Society in 1853. Curiously, however, no images or pictures of Benjamin W. Corlies, a prominent citizen, have been found.

The first U.S. Federal Census containing details about the family of Benjamin W. Corlies was that of 1850, which shows them living in Ocean Township. This is consistent with the formation of Ocean Township the previous year (Eatontown was then part of what became Ocean Township). Corlies was quite prosperous for the time—a "farmer" with property valued at $20,000. Subsequent census records for 1870 and 1880 also list Corlies as a farmer.

Genealogical information provides more details about his life, including mention of the fiftieth wedding anniversary celebration he shared with his wife, Miriam (Tilton), in 1870. The certificate memorializing the occasion, a Quaker tradition, is now at the Monmouth County Historical Association.

Six months before he died, and perhaps in failing health, Benjamin W. Corlies sold his estate on "the south side of the Eatontown and Sea Shore Turnpike (Broadway)" to Mathew Byrnes. Corlies likely retained other real estate and may have moved there.

When Benjamin W. Corlies finally succumbed to a stroke in May 1884, his obituary incorrectly listed his middle initial as "J." His wife of fifty-six years, Miriam T. Corlies, predeceased him in 1876. Five of their children were living when Benjamin died. Before his death, the lifelong Quaker was an elder in the Shrewsbury Friends' Meeting.

Benjamin W. Corlies's last will and testament is dated February 13, 1882. In it, he bequeaths money and other valuables to his children. No specific mention is made of how he wished to dispose of his real estate, which may be why court-appointed administrators divided his remaining real estate among his heirs in November 1888.

The 1880 U.S. Federal Census lists Francis Corlies (Benjamin W. Corlies's fourth child) as a "surveyor." Could this be a case of "like father, like son?"

As previously shown in the Monmouth County Historical Association genealogical records, Francis Corlies died in 1897. His obituary reveals the final proof we need about his father. It reads: "Son of Benjamin W. Corlies, who was one of the foremost surveyors of Monmouth County in his day."

Thus, the weight of all this evidence makes it reasonable to conclude that the "BWC" initials on the January 1849 map refer to Benjamin W. Corlies, an Eatontown resident who drew it to illustrate the separation of Ocean Township from Shrewsbury Township.

—From *New Jersey Studies: An Interdisciplinary Journal,* Summer 2018

21

The Quaker Abolition Movement

By Rick Geffken

T he unfortunate truth is that slavery was everywhere in the early United States—not just in the southern states. Enslaved people were held—obviously, against their will—for over two hundred years in New Jersey. The largest individual slaveholder in East Jersey was Lewis Morris (1601–1691), who brought over sixty slaves with him from Barbados to Tinton Falls between 1676 and 1679. He called his plantation Tintern Manor. When he died, Morris owned 57 percent of all the slaves in East New Jersey, according to Colgate University historian Graham Russell Hodges.

Because Morris—and eventually his heir and nephew, also named Lewis Morris (1671–1746)—owned thousands of acres of farmland in Monmouth County, their embrace of slavery provided a virtual imprimatur for others to embrace slavery as an acceptable practice. When the younger Lewis Morris became the first colonial governor of the state in 1738, he likely brought some enslaved people to Trenton with him.

Although exact figures will probably never be known, scholars suggest that the number of black people in New Jersey, mostly all slaves, increased from 200 in 1680 to 12,422 (about 6 percent of the total population) in the 1800 census. In actuality, the number was probably higher. That number gradually decreased until slavery was finally abolished by the Thirteenth Amendment to the U.S. Constitution. New Jersey was the last northern state to ratify it (in January 1866).

In the two-hundred-year interim between the time Morris's enslaved workers arrived in Monmouth County and New Jersey's ratification of the Thirteenth Amendment, Quakers were lobbying for an end to this inhuman institution, often referred to as "America's Original Sin."

As early as 1672, the founder of the Society of Friends, George Fox, had specifically addressed this issue during a visit to the budding Shrewsbury Quaker community in East Jersey. In *Keeping Up the Gospel Order*, Fox wrote:

> *If you were in the same condition as the Blacks are…now I say, if this should be the condition of you and yours, you would think it hard measure, yea, and very great Bondage and Cruelty. And therefore consider seriously of this, and do you for and to them, as you would willingly have them or any other to do unto you…were you in the like slavish condition.*

In his November 23, 1683 will, Shrewsbury Quaker Meeting founding member Richard Lippincott bequeathed his younger slaves to his children but chose to free his older slaves. Six years later, his son John Lippincott sold part of his inherited land in Shrewsburytown to the Quaker community. This property, located at the corner of Broad Street and Sycamore Avenue, is still owned by the Society of Friends. The current meetinghouse—the cedar shake–sided building listed in the state and national registries of historic places—was erected in 1816.

Shrewsbury Quakers opposed the importation of slaves into New Jersey in 1730. In 1757, they disowned John Wardell, who lived just across the Four Corners from the meetinghouse, for buying a slave. The next year, the Quakers asked their members to stop buying slaves, to teach literacy to slave children and to free their slaves once they reached the age of twenty-one. In 1778, Quaker John Corlies (and his mother, Zilpha) were "read out" of the meeting due to "his keeping Negroes in Slavery."

The influential Quaker abolitionist John Woolman, from Mount Holly, spoke at the Shrewsbury Meeting in 1761 during one of his many preaching forays throughout New Jersey. Some years earlier, Woolman wrote about the consequences of keeping people enslaved and foresaw the Civil War:

> *If the white people retain a resolution to prefer their outward prospects of gain to all other considerations, and do not act conscientiously toward [slaves] as fellow-creatures, I believe that burden will grow heavier and heavier, until times change in a way disagreeable to us.*

A 1771 list of slaveholders in Shrewsbury totals ninety-seven slaves held by fifty-eight slaveholders. At least a quarter of these slaveholders were Quakers, including members of prominent and well-off families like the Parkers and the Wardells. To their credit, some Parker family members manumitted enslaved people a few years later, during the Revolutionary War. In January 1778, Josiah Parker "set free from bondage my Negro man Joseph…[and] my Negro boy Samuel."

One of the most fascinating stories from the Revolutionary period concerns an enslaved man owned by the aforementioned John Corlies. Corlies took out a newspaper ad in November 1775 offering a reward of three pounds for the return of "a NEGROE man, named Titus, but will probably change his name." No one claimed the reward, because Titus appears to have fled to Virginia, where the British governor, Lord Dunmore, was offering freedom to runaways joining his "Ethiopian Regiment."

After training with Dunmore, Titus returned home, calling himself Colonel Tye (as Corlies had predicted, he had changed his moniker), and led a series of raids throughout Monmouth County. Leading black troops from British-occupied Sandy Hook, Tye fought in the Battle of Monmouth in 1778. Two years later, he was wounded during an attack on Joshua Huddy's house in Colts Neck, contracted an infection and died. There is no evidence that Tye wreaked revenge on Corlies, specifically, although one suspects that might have been a partial motive for his Shrewsbury depredations during the war.

All of these Quaker exhortations and actions eventually paid off. By 1780, few Shrewsbury Quakers were slaveholders. During the tumultuous eighteenth century, New Jersey lawmakers took note of the growing abolition movement and made painfully gradual steps toward freeing slaves from bondage. A 1714 law was intended to look like it supported freeing slaves but added the onerous provision that the freeing slaveholder must submit an initial £200—and £20 per year—for the freed person. Asking farmers and small merchants to pay what would have been the equivalent of $42,000 in today's money, and another $4,200 every year, would preclude manumissions. This ridiculous law was repealed in 1798.

The 1804 Act for the Gradual Abolition of Slavery was another "give with one hand and take with the other" piece of legislation. Among its provisions was one that stipulated freedom for children born after July 4, 1804, but with the proviso that females were required "to serve" their masters until they became twenty-one. Male slaves had to wait until they were twenty-five to gain real freedom.

The Quaker meetinghouse at Broad Street and Sycamore Avenue in Shrewsbury was built in 1816. *Dorn's Classic Images.*

This is precisely what happened to Charles Reeves, according to research done by his great-granddaughter Amanda Mae Edwards, who was eighty-six years old in 2019. Reeves was born in May 1820, enslaved to David Williamson of Middletown and waited until 1845 to be manumitted. His wife, Hannah B. Van Cleaf, was also freed before they married around 1851. Edwards is rightly proud that she is the third generation descended from Reeves to live and prosper in the Lincroft section of Middletown.

The New Jersey State Constitution of 1844 unequivocally said, "all men are free and independent," although the New Jersey Supreme Court subsequently ruled that this essentially meant white men. Two years later, what appeared to be a law abolishing slavery was passed and freed all black children born after its passage, but the state's few existing slaves remained "apprentices for life." It might have made some white people feel good about themselves, but black people hardly had reason to celebrate.

After the Civil War, New Jersey was, alas, the last northern state to agree with the Thirteenth Amendment's abolition of slavery. Even then, it did so begrudgingly. When the amendment had been ratified by three-fourths of the states by 1866, New Jersey was forced to abide by it. The New Jersey Constitutional Convention of 1875 finally conformed the state constitution with the post–Civil War amendments (including the Fourteenth and Fifteenth).

The Society of Friends was a conscience and moral guide for citizens until the final throes of slavery in the United States. The Shrewsbury Quakers stand among the tallest of these.

In fairness to the Garden State, New Jersey was among the first to officially apologize for slavery in a resolution passed by its legislature in 2008:

> *The Legislature of the State of New Jersey expressed its profound regret for the State's role in slavery and apologizes for the wrong inflicted by slavery and its after effects in the United States of America; expresses its deepest sympathies and solemn regrets to those who were enslaved and the descendants of those slaves, who were deprived of life, human dignity, and the constitutional protections accorded all citizens of the United States; and we encourage all citizens to remember and teach their children about the history of slavery, Jim Crow laws, and modern day slavery, to ensure that these tragedies will neither be forgotten nor repeated.*

—Previously unpublished

Part III: Old Middletown

22

LINCROFT'S HIDDEN CEMETERY

By Muriel J. Smith

A Monmouth University professor and her students are leading the way to restore a long-forgotten nineteenth-century cemetery to a fitting resting place for the African Americans buried there.

What was designed as a social work project for a Monmouth University class is now a countywide undertaking involving at least two churches, Boy Scouts, Monmouth County Historical Commission representatives, the Monmouth County Historical Association, the Middletown Township Landmarks Commission and dozens of volunteers working to restore a sense of history and pride.

Cedar Hill Cemetery is located off Hurley's Lane, directly behind St. Leo the Great Catholic Church. Once a proud and well cared-for final resting place for families who purchased large individual burial plots, it has remained untouched and unnoticed, for the most part, since it was last tended in the 1940s. Seven decades later, all that could be seen was a large expanse of hilly turf completely covered with downed trees, brambling bushes, uneven topography, crowded new growth of grass and the damaged, fallen, crushed, and—up until now—forgotten grave markers of those buried there.

Joelle M. Zabotka, PhD, assistant professor at Monmouth University's School of Social Work, outlined the project, which has been in the planning and orientation stages for months. The cemetery houses the remains of what could be one hundred African American family members, many of whom fought in the Civil War and were from families of freed slaves in Monmouth County.

Zabotka heard of the forgotten cemetery through Monmouth County Historic Commission member Maureen O'Connor Leach, who had spoken with a couple she saw carrying a U.S. flag on Memorial Day, 2015, looking for veterans to honor. Zabotka determined that a practical lesson for her students would be to discover the identities and lives of those buried in the cemetery, and the project was launched within a month. An outline was prepared, and clean-up began in October 2015. By the time the next college term began, the project was expanded to include a program at St. Leo's Church. The program included Monmouth University faculty members, including Zabotka, along with historian Joseph A. Grabas and Leach, explaining the project and the cemetery to groups of interested followers.

At the start of the project, Monmouth University students visited the site, uncovered many names and birthdates on the stones and were divided into teams, with each assigned to learn more about their subjects. Students were delegated to begin the arduous task of restoring the cemetery.

Adding to the mystery of the project is the actual ownership of the property. Research by historian Joseph A. Grabas, a member of the county historic commission, shows that the plots were sold to individual owners rather than it being an entire cemetery tended by a church. In 1958, the Catholic Diocese of Trenton purchased two adjoining chicken farms and built St. Leo the Great, followed by the school, on twenty acres. Since neither burial grounds nor churches pay taxes, the lines separating the properties are unclear, as is specific ownership.

Ray Veth, a member of the Middletown Landmarks Commission and the township's Save Our Cemeteries Committee who has considerable experience with recovering and cleaning up other historic burial grounds in the township, was also on hand that Saturday in June 2015 when the clean-up began. During the initial work of laying out the original plot plans, determining where the row of trees separating the grounds from adjacent property were located and helping to identify the people named on the stones, Veth wanted to be certain the project was proceeding within the commission's guidelines. Later, Veth said, "This is an outstanding plan. I would not change a thing. It is quite an undertaking, but many hands make light work. Thanks to Dr. Zabotka and all of her efforts in coordinating the cleanup."

Veth, who also owns a trophy and sign shop in Middletown, offered to donate a sign for the perimeter of the property and said he would work with adjacent property owners to determine the best location. He added he would be happy to help students with their genealogical research and will keep the Middletown Historic Society informed about the progress.

Students have already begun their research, with some using the records at the Monmouth County Historical Association, which is also ready to assist with tracing histories through its resources. Some have connected with fourth-generation descendants of the deceased, while others have been stymied in their research because of the young age of the deceased and not having any recorded records of land purchases, marriages or progeny.

Grabas spent Saturday morning walking the grounds with Zabotka, comparing the stones they and the Boy Scouts from Lincroft Troop 110

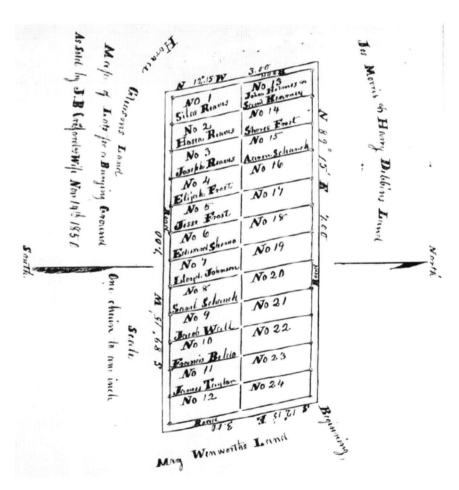

The descendants of many of the African Americans buried in the Cedar Hill Cemetery have lived in the Lincroft section of Middletown for two centuries. *Joseph A. Grabas.*

uncovered and photographing plots from several tax maps drawn at different times in the twentieth century. Grabas said each of the plots purchased by individuals and families was large—approximately one hundred by forty feet—and more than one hundred persons could be buried in each plot.

According to an 1850 deed, Grabas said, a property owner named Crawford sold the land as twenty-four individual plots to a group of African Americans in the area known as Leedsville in the mid-nineteenth century. Grabas presented Zabotka with several maps and helped the students with their research.

Grabas noted that records in the Middletown Township Public Library refer to efforts by Judy Norris in 1979 to document the gravestones when the property was known as the Reeves Burial Ground. There are other references to it as Cedar View Cemetery, Lincroft Cemetery and Hurley's Woods Burial Ground. Grabas indicated it could also be known as the Alexander Frost Burial Ground, referring to the main proponent of the cemetery, who purchased it and sold remaining plots to other individuals or families. Frost also purchased three acres of land from John B. Crawford in 1839.

To add another dimension to the mysteries surrounding the cemetery, Grabas said, "It would be interesting to explore the relationship between Crawford, a former slaveowner, and Frost. Was he Crawford's manumitted slave? Why would a former slave owner convey land to 'coloured men'?"

The stones themselves, most of which are simple granite with names and some life information inscribed on them, tell the beginnings of the stories of the men and women who were most likely former slaves freed during or after the Civil War. Some bear the inscriptions of "Private, USCT CO. B," which Grabas indicated was the soldier's rank in the U.S. Colored Troops and his military company during the war. Some list the deceased's parents and dates of birth and death, and some note that the stone was "erected by a friend." Some of the names of the deceased are not the names of the owners who purchased the plots, Grabas explains, indicating the possibility that they were purchased by one person and either donated to or sold to someone else.

Joe Manzi, director of finance and operations for St. Leo, was also at the field work Saturday, congratulating Zabotka on the intensity and direction of the project and indicating the parish's interest and cooperation in seeing the deceased remembered and their resting places restored.

Zabotka said nearby Calvary Baptist Church has also shown keen interest in and support of the project, although no records show that any of the plots were connected with any specific church. Many of the tombstones already uncovered show death dates in the 1870s and 1880s, with the most recent in the early 1900s. At least one of the births, that of Emaline Schanck, is dated 1839, and another, that of John Anthony Holmes, is December 21, 1818. Silas Reeves, a private in U.S. Colored Troops Company B, Forty-First Regiment, was born in 1845 and died in 1910.

"This is an exciting project for everybody involved," Zabotka said. "What better way to teach social work than to uncover the lives and histories of people?"

The professor noted that while early work on restoration and renovations is extremely limited until the volunteers and students under her direction can locate and identify every stone in the burying ground, "we will welcome volunteers at some time in the future to help clean the area and restore its appearance as a true burial ground." Despite the efforts of so many historians and family members, as of 2019, it remained an ongoing effort to keep the grounds clean.

—From the *Two River Times*, October 29, 2015

23

LINCROFT LEGACY

By Rick Geffken

T he Cedar View Cemetery in Lincroft has been called the Reeves Burial Ground for good reason—many of the souls lying in repose there are descendants of two formerly enslaved people, Charles Reeves and Hannah Van Cleaf, who were both manumitted under the 1804 New Jersey Act for the Gradual Abolition of Slavery.

Charles Reeves was born to unknown parents in May 1820 on the Middletown farm of David Williamson. The 1804 law required that any male slave born after the Fourth of July that year "serve" their owners for twenty-five years before attaining freedom; females were to "serve" for twenty-one years. The legislation was one of many New Jersey attempts to right the historic wrong of slavery while simultaneously protecting the property of slaveholders.

Hannah Van Cleaf was born in February 1828 in Middletown. Various historic documents list enslaved people with the same Dutch last name, so Hannah or her forebears may once have been owned by Van Cleafs (or Van Cleves). Charles and Hannah married around 1850, just a few years before the Williamson farm became part of the new township of Holmdel. According to their great-granddaughter and Riverview Hospital retired nurse Amanda Mae (Smack) Edwards, Charles and Hannah had eleven children between 1845 and 1872.

Within a year of the marriage, the freeman Charles Reeves began working on the farm of Garrett D. Hendrickson, one of a multigenerational family of Dutch slaveholders. Hendrickson was also a cousin of David Williamson's wife, Phebe Hendrickson.

Charles Reeves was born enslaved in 1820; his descendants lived in his Lincroft home for almost a century. *Amanda Mae (Smack) Edwards.*

By 1870, after Garrett Hendrickson died, Charles Reeves was hired by George W. Crawford of Middletown. His new employer must have especially revered Reeves—he gave the African American man and his family a house, which was moved from what is now the Christian Brothers Academy property to Middletown-Lincroft Road. Four generations of Reeves lived in that Lincroft home.

According to Ed Raser in his definitive *New Jersey Graveyard & Gravestone Inscriptions Locators: Monmouth County*, "On 14 November 1850, John B. Crawford, a wealthy area farmer, and former slave owner, for $60, sold a 2.05-acre tract to 14 black men 'to be used for a buying ground.'" Three of the fourteen men were brothers: Elijah, Jesse and Alexander Frost. Alexander later sold a cemetery plot to Charles Reeves.

Why Crawford sold land to African Americans, some of whom were former slaves, has never been fully explained. The conventions and practices of eighteenth- and nineteenth-century slaveholders may offer a clue to this rare transaction. Crawford's son George was married to a white woman named Sarah Frost. It's possible that the black Frosts who purchased cemetery plots had once been enslaved to white Frosts and took their family name. Or, as often happened to enslaved women, they bore children as a result of sexual relations, whether by choice or not, with their owners. In either case, the cemetery plot sale seems to be a recognition of the affection the white Crawford and Frost families had for the people who spent years of "faithful service" to them. Until written proof—if it exists—surfaces, this is purely speculative but nonetheless an intriguing possibility.

When Charles Reeves passed away in 1900, his obituary in the *Red Bank Register* read: "Mr. Reeves was one of the best-known colored men in Middletown township. He was a member of the Baptist church at Red Bank, and for thirty-three years had rarely missed a Sunday. After his marriage he and his wife walked from Lincroft to Red Bank every Sunday morning, returning home at noon, and he would go alone to church every Sunday night. In later years he was able to buy a horse with which he and his wife went to church, and after he got the horse the children became regular attendants."

Hannah lived another two decades before dying in 1918. The couple rest side by side in the little Lincroft cemetery, so long neglected, beneath matching black granite stones. Simply engraved with just their names and dates, the markers were lovingly carved and put in place years later by their son Charles Reeves Jr.

—Previously unpublished

24

DONALD DE LUE,
LEONARDO SCULPTOR

By Muriel J. Smith

His *Rocket Thrower* is in Flushing Meadows in Queens; his *Boy Scout Memorial* is in President's Park in Washington, D.C.; one of his *George Washington* statues is in Lansing, Michigan; another is in Indiana; and still another, *Kneeling in Prayer*, is in Paramus. There is no doubt that Donald De Lue was a master of sculpture and an artist recognized in his own time who will be revered forever after.

In August 2018, it was thirty years since Donald De Lue died, but there are many in the Bayshore who still remember and respect the soft-spoken, gentle man who lived and created many of his magnificent works at his home and studio at 82 Highland Avenue in Leonardo.

De Lue was born Donald Harcourt Quigley but took on a maternal family name when he was twenty-one years old. He was born in Boston and studied there, as well as in New York and Paris, under many famous sculptors and artists of his day. He had a style and flair all his own, to say nothing of his energy and dedication to hard work. In a career that spanned a half-century, he created hundreds of statutes, medals and medallions, many of them patriotic and many of them epitomizing the virtues of strength, patriotism, energy and the American spirit. In an interview he gave in his Leonardo studio in 1975, De Lue said his mission was to "give dignity to the man, not make a hero of De Lue."

His statue of Thomas Jefferson, which was created from two tons of clay, says it all. Commissioned by the Bicentennial Commission of Jefferson Parish, Louisiana, the clay model was created in Leonardo, and later cast in bronze in New York and set on a Dakota mahogany granite base in the heart of a new plaza in Metairie, Louisiana, a lasting tribute to the man who made the Louisiana Purchase a reality. The sculptor said he created the eight-foot-six-inch-tall statue—complete with smile wrinkles on the president's jaw and furrows in his brow—to show both the strength and gentleness of Jefferson.

Facial features showing emotions and feelings became an important element of his work as De Lue fashioned all the greats he has molded in clay in a studio cluttered with drawings, sketches, piles of books and assorted other items he deemed important to his work.

Leonardo-based sculptor Donald De Lue created monumental statues of famous people and iconic images. *Gettysburg Sculptures.*

The clay model was the one later cast in plaster, which created the mold to be filled with plaster and cast in bronze in New York, then shipped to Louisiana for formal dedication ceremonies. The model was actually started long before, at the time when the sculptor first put pen to paper for his initial ideas. De Lue had read numerous books about Jefferson to get more insight into his personality, then pored over every drawing done during the president's lifetime—he wanted to ensure his dimensions were accurate in creating a statue one and a half times Jefferson's size. It was only then that he created the steel frame in which he would wrap the clay. Although he destroyed the model once the plaster cast was made, De Lue used the clay again for yet another purpose.

The master artist never took count of the number of works he created, nor did he remember which was his first. He lived for the next one he would make and always said his last one was his favorite. His sculptures, testimonies to his great talent, are located throughout the United States and in many other countries in diverse locations such as churches, convents, museums, colleges and universities. His *Athlete* is at the Naval Academy in Annapolis, his Boy Scout Memorial is in Washington and his *Dr. Martin Luther King* is at Wichita State University in Kansas. A sculpture of *Eagles* is at the U.S. Courthouse in Philadelphia, and another *Washington Kneeling in Prayer* is at the Freedom Foundation at Valley Forge. A De Lue sculpture is at the U.S. Battle

Monument in Normandy, France, and several of his works are at Gettysburg National Military Park.

The *Rocket Thrower* is one of the largest—if not the largest—of all of De Lue's works. Created for the New York World's Fair in 1964, it is forty-five feet high, cast in bronze, and was one of the earliest concepts of man's relationship to space and an adventurous spirit. Although he was not selected by the sculpture committee to create a statue for the fair, De Lue went to the committee and requested he be included. He was, and he was given six months to create his masterpiece. He did, completing it in time to be shipped to Italy for casting. He was allocated $105,000 for the statue, which still stands on the grounds of the World's Fair in Flushing. He envisioned his works lasting for thousands of years.

De Lue and his wife, Naomi, lived in Leonardo even while he maintained other studios in New York and Italy. He gave one-man shows of his work at both Monmouth University and Brookdale Community College and displayed more than two dozen of his sculptures and medallions at Bell Labs in Holmdel. Naomi died in 1982, and Donald died in his sleep in Leonardo six years later, with his last work, *The Leper*, remaining unfinished. Both Donald and Naomi are buried in Old Bridge.

—From the *Atlantic Highlands Journal*, June 16, 2018

25

PEACE, HARMONY AND CIVIL WAR IN MIDDLETOWN

By Rick Geffken

For the past sixteen years, Civil War reenactors representing the Third New Jersey Volunteers have held a weekend encampment at the Heath Farm in Middletown. They perform training drills and demonstrate and discuss how their real-life counterparts and support personnel carried out their military duties. And, as soldiers always do, they sit around and gripe about the war and army food. Where they do all this is part of a remarkable story.

The original Third New Jersey Volunteers broke training camp in Trenton in the spring of 1861 on their way to significant battles such as Bull Run (also known as First Manassas). Later, they were at Second Bull Run, Antietam and Gettysburg in July 1863. There's no record showing Clinton Heath interacting with the original Third New Jersey during the Civil War, but he certainly benefited from the successful outcome of bloodiest war ever fought on American soil.

By 1894, Clinton P. Heath, who was born enslaved at New Bern, North Carolina, was farming the fifty acres of prime land he bought in Middletown. Current family matriarch Susie Spradley, a Heath relative through marriage, still lives on the property while maintaining her family's legacy. She and her children and grandchildren welcomed the Third New Jersey detachment to the farm on Saturday, September 10, 2016.

Heath's emancipation and subsequent journey to New Jersey as a freeman allowed him to start as a tenant farmer, buy land, marry, build a home,

Bob Mataranglo painted *The Gatekeeper*, honoring Clinton P. Heath, on a building at the Middletown farm still owned by Heath's descendants. *Keith Maidlow.*

and raise a large and prosperous family. Clinton Heath was said to be a man who could get two crops for every one other tenant farmers produced. To supplement his seasonal income, he worked on the railroad for forty years. The Ku Klux Klan held meetings not too far from Heath's home in Middletown during his lifetime, making his achievements as a black man here even more notable.

Among the twenty or so Third New Jersey reenactors present on this particular Saturday were riflemen, a field surgeon, drill instructors, an engineering detachment and several women representing musicians and cooks. Officers' wives would travel to battlefields to visit their husbands during the Civil War, with rank always having its personal privileges.

Civil War reenactors spend years and their own money researching diaries and accumulating Civil War records and books so they can portray soldiers as accurately as possible. In addition to initial outfitting costs of around $1,500, the men and women depicting nineteenth-century military personnel pay all their own travel and meeting costs while pursuing their hobby.

Dr. Allan Hordof, a retired pediatric cardiologist at New York–Presbyterian University Hospital of Columbia and Cornell, was a natural choice to act as a field surgeon. He explained, "Most of the medical professionals drafted during the Civil War were what we'd call today general practitioners. Surgery was rare at the time and many of the techniques they pioneered at field hospitals helped develop surgical training after the war." He also spoke about the depictions of doctors holding down wounded troops while they hacked off limbs in classic movies like *Gone with the Wind* or in more recent films like *Glory*. "There was obviously blood and gore in the war, but most of those film scenes were just Hollywood theater." Dr. Hordof continued, "Chloroform and ether were known in the 1840s, but their massive use happened during the war. You need a cooperative patient. You can't saw off an arm if the patient is jumping around the table in front of you—they were given an anesthetic before drastic surgery and were out cold during most operations."

Dr. John St. Peter, a former principal in the Middletown school system, is one of the prominent reenactors with the Third New Jersey. When he was a history teacher, Dr. St. Peter introduced his grammar-school students to as much local history as he could each school year. "It wouldn't be allowed today, of course," St. Peter recalls, "but with five chaperones, we took my classes on overnight field trips to places like the Spy House in Port Monmouth."

Ironically, when the Monmouth County Park System restored the Spy House and renamed it the Seabrook-Wilson House, many of its artifacts went to the Heath Farm. They were sent there because Walter Spradley, the grandson of Clinton Heath, was interested in Middletown history and agreed to build a museum on the Heath Farm. A U.S. Army veteran who had retired after running multiple businesses, Spradley had the artifacts legally transferred to make sure they stayed in Middletown.

Walter's aunt Bertha was a determined woman who took it upon herself to preserve the Heath Farm. Bertha Clara Heath was Clinton's youngest daughter and the last of his thirteen children. She graduated from Harlem Hospital School of Nursing in 1930, went on to earn her BS at New York University, and received a master of science degree from Columbia University. She worked as a registered nurse until retiring in 1974.

Bertha Heath spent her remaining years working with Walter and his wife, Susie Spradley, to safeguard the remaining ten-acre section of her father's original holdings. Some sections of the original farm went to relatives; others were sold for residential and commercial development. Bertha couldn't bear to see her family's historic property entirely disappear, so she established a family trust called the Bertha Clara Heath Foundation to help preserve as much as possible. She and her nephew Walter collected and catalogued family artifacts, which now share display space with articles from the Spy House.

Mary Ann and Keith Maidlow met and befriended Walter Spradley in 1999, when they were living on Heath Parkway, which was carved out of the original homestead. Enthralled by Walter's wisdom and enthusiasm for people and local history, they've devoted years to working with Walter and Susie as cocurators of the exhibits at Heath Farm.

Susie Spradley recalled that "Mary Ann knew Dr. St. Peter when her children were in school, and because he was a history buff, she introduced us, and he brought his students here. Later on, he had the idea to bring the Civil War reenactors." As often happens, these convergences led to long-lasting friendships and community.

Dr. St. Peter added: "They say blood is thicker than water, but sometimes good friends are even thicker than blood. Walter touched all of us during the time he was alive and welcomed us here on his farm. He was just a charismatic, down-to-earth guy."

Keith Maidlow remembered Walter Spradley as "an engaging man who often told me, 'We don't own anything here; we're just keeping it safe for our children.' He would get so proud and chest-pumped when the Third New Jersey showed up every year."

Walter used to say that the Heath Farm was the best-kept secret in Middletown. Judging by the few visitors on this particular Saturday, that's still true. Susie Spradley and the Maidlows hope to change that. Information can be found on Facebook by searching for "The Historic Heath Farm." The Third New Jersey Volunteers maintain a website at http://www.3rdnj.org/.

Bertha Heath died in 1998. Walter Spradley passed away in 2014. At the event on Saturday, September 10, 2016, Walter's widow, Susie, lovingly looked on as her children and grandchildren worked and played exactly where their family has lived for over 130 years. The newest generation spent this past year building a henhouse and beehives and planting new trees. Susie feels confident the family legacy will continue.

The Heath and Spradley community involvement and generosity of spirit were felt everywhere at Saturday's encampment—an African American family hosting and feeding white Civil War reenactors at a historic farm located on the corner of Harmony Road and Peace Lane.

—From the *Two River Times*, September 22–29, 2016

REVOLUTIONARY MIDDLETOWN

By Rick Geffken

One hundred and some odd years after it was established in 1664, Middletown was the scene of several crucial events in the Revolutionary War. A recently passed New Jersey state bill signed into law by Governor (and Middletown resident) Phil Murphy on August 17, 2018, may bring renewed attention to the physical location of events that occurred in and around one of the three original townships in Monmouth County (Freehold and Shrewsbury were the other two).

Named after New Jersey Assembly speaker Craig Coughlin, the Coughlin Bill "requires the New Jersey Historical Commission to establish a program to observe the 250th anniversary of United States independence, and the state's first Constitution."

The few roadside plaques commemorating disparate incidents between 1776 and 1883 hardly seem sufficient. "There is much to celebrate about New Jersey. This is a wonderful opportunity to expand the narrative about New Jersey, and let others know the contributions we made to the formation of America," said Speaker Coughlin.

It remains to be seen if and how Middletown Township will take advantage of the Coughlin Bill to draw more attention to its early history.

Reflecting on the mere $500,000 appropriated in the Coughlin Bill for creating commemorative programs, Randall Gabrielan of the Middletown Historical Society (he is also a Monmouth County Historical Commission member) said, "One hopes the state will be as motivated to preserve their neglected historic properties along with their desire to celebrate. Many need urgent attention." Another Monmouth County Historical Commission member, Don Burden, hopes that "the passage of this legislation will be the impetus for planning an event of commemoration for the 250th anniversary [of the country]."

Now known as a suburban enclave for families and a bedroom community for working commuters, Middletown was the scene of more than a few

Old First Church on King's Highway in Middletown is the oldest Baptist church in New Jersey. *Dorn's Classic Images.*

Revolutionary War incidents. In May 1777, the congregation of Old First Church on King's Highway, the oldest Baptist church in New Jersey, was engaged in a fierce debate over which side to favor. Church elders settled the matter, according to church historian Elaine Lent, who discovered an extraordinary document just a few years ago. The letter made clear that the Old First Church would support the Whigs (now referred to as "Patriots") and throw out Loyalist members.

After the Battle of Monmouth (Court House) in June 1778, retreating British troops journeyed along Kings Highway, then through Chapel Hill and Buttermilk Valley on their way to evacuation ships in Sandy Hook Bay. Just down the road from Old First Baptist, Marlpit Hall was the home of Edward Taylor, who joined in the resistance to British policies before the war. Ultimately, however, he remained a Loyalist, was arrested and died just before the Treaty of Paris ended the war in 1783. Marlpit Hall survives to this day and is operated as a museum by the Monmouth County Historical Association.

In the period between these two well-known events, the first, and rarely noted, Revolutionary War battle in Monmouth County occurred

Marlpit Hall, home of Loyalist Edward Taylor, survives to this day as a museum operated by the Monmouth County Historical Association. *Monmouth County Historical Association.*

in Middletown. During the Battle of Navesink Highlands, about one hundred and seventy British troops attacked Patriot militia stationed at the Hartshorne House in February 1777. Twenty-five Patriots were killed, and seventy-two officers and men were captured. Among the former were men with prominent Monmouth County names like Crawford; included in the latter were a Stillwell and a Goodenough.

Just a few summers ago, Dr. Richard Veit of Monmouth University led an archaeological dig at the base of the Sandy Hook Lighthouse. He and his students were seeking remnants of the "Refugee Town" located there during the Revolution. The Loyalists living on Sandy Hook frequently raided Middletown and other bayside communities for supplies and foodstuffs.

Of course, much has been written about the famous hanging of Patriot Joshua Huddy in Highlands in 1782. But when the British strung him up at Gravelly Point (Loyalists pinned a note to his chest that read "Up goes Huddy for Phillip White"—a story for another time), Highlands was a part of Middletown.

An intriguing aspect of the Coughlin Bill is the establishment of a commission that "will be authorized to enter into a public-private partnership agreement with a private entity to plan and undertake the historical activities and programs." Tax-exempt nonprofits have until 2033 to apply for some of the $500,000 appropriated for creating commemorative programs. This means that enterprising local entities have an opportunity to join with Middletown to maintain and administer national heritage areas within the township.

—From the *Two River Times*, September 13, 2018

27

Stone Church in Navesink

By Muriel J. Smith

It was October 1861 when Dr. William N. Dunnell, rector of Trinity Church in Red Bank, thought would be a good idea to have weeknight church services in the village of Riceville, as Navesink was called in the nineteenth century. The services were held in the schoolhouse behind the library. At first, they were held once a month, then twice a month, and before long, on one Sunday per month, as well.

A strong belief in God and a desire to have a church of their own were strong among the families in Navesink. So, when Charles Milnor decided to gather his children and neighbors together for teaching catechism some nine months after Dr. Dunnell's first service, a few youngsters attended. The next class, a few more showed up, and before long, there were seventy youngsters being taught by the women of the Milnor family and other neighborhood ladies. The All Saints Sunday School was well established!

Mrs. James Edgar was an early churchgoer and dreamed of having a chapel built, a dream she could not fulfill before her death. However, her wish was carried out by her father, John Stephens, and her husband, together with other family members, who built All Saints as a memorial to her and other deceased family members.

Nine days short of Dr. Dunnell's first service, on October 7, 1863, the cornerstone of All Saints Memorial Church was laid in the Highlands of Navesink. Less than a year later, a parochial organization was formed, and the new building was consecrated.

All Saints Memorial Church, commonly known as Stone Church, is English Gothic Revival in style and built of peanut stone. *Muriel J. Smith.*

Family names among the founders are still familiar in Navesink and the surrounding area: Milnor, Hartshorne, Stephens, Sickles, Carhart. The church and its community have grown and become an integral part of the area.

In its growth and expansion, All Saints reaches out to the community in numerous ways in addition to offering open invitations to attend Sunday services. The Stone Church Players, a community theater group, stages musicals, classics, comedies, radio plays and holiday programs and celebrated the tenth anniversary of this ministry in 2018.

The All Saints Memorial Church Cemetery is the final resting place for many of the founding families of All Saints, along with other local families. When St. Andrews Church, originally known as the Old Reformed Church of Highlands, was closed, the graves from that church were reinterred in All Saints Cemetery with an obelisk to commemorate the deceased. Three years ago, remains from the Memorial Garden at Fair Haven's Church of the Holy Communion were also recommitted to the cemetery. A memorial garden has been included for the interment of cremation ashes as All Saints continues to meet the needs of the community.

The church has numerous ministries, including men's, women's and youth groups; Garden Angels, who tend the landscaping on the church grounds; the cemetery ministry; and others.

All of this proves that All Saints Church of the Highlands of Navesink is still the same thriving, bustling, intricate part of the community that it has been from the very beginning.

—From the *Atlantic Highlands Journal*, December 12, 2017

PART IV: WESTERN MONMOUTH

28

BEN SHAHN PAINTS ROOSEVELT

By Muriel J. Smith

On the wall of the entry lobby at the Roosevelt Elementary School, spread forty-five feet across the wall and rising a magnificent twelve feet is Ben Shahn's story of the immigration of Eastern Europeans to the United States in the early part of the twentieth century. The story, a fresco the social realist painted when commissioned to do so by the federal Farm Security Administration in 1936, depicts in stark realism the struggle Eastern European Jews faced, the battles they had to fight and the settlement they designed that created a community and made a new, happier life possible in a new homeland.

First called the Jersey Homesteads, the town of Roosevelt, carved out of Millstone in western Monmouth County, was one of ninety-nine communities created as part of President Franklin Roosevelt's New Deal initiative. In appreciation of the community, the only one of the ninety-nine to be planned as an agro-industrial cooperative for urban Jewish garment workers in New York, the residents changed the name to Roosevelt after the president's death in 1945.

Ben Shahn had never been to Roosevelt before he accepted the job in 1936. An immigrant from Lithuania, Shahn was eight when his mother brought him and his siblings to the United States in 1906 to reunite with his father, who had had been exiled from the Russian Empire country and managed to get to the United States. The family lived in New York, and Shahn was apprenticed to a lithographer during his teenage years, entering New York University when he was nineteen and later studying with the

The New Jersey borough was named for Franklin D. Roosevelt after his death on April 12, 1945. *Muriel J. Smith.*

National Academy of Design. He traveled extensively to Europe and Africa, painting and studying with other masters and staging his first one-man show in New York in 1929.

In creating the mural, the purpose of which was to visually explain the foundation of the Jersey Homesteads, Shahn used the medium of fresco, or painting done on moist plaster with color pigments dissolved in water, the art form he had learned from Mexican artist Diego Rivera. Rivera was also a social realist and influenced Shahn's political views, which were often displayed in the works he created either for specific commissions or for sale. Art historians also believe the Roosevelt mural not only tells the story of the Monmouth County community but is the artist's own Haggadah, the Jewish tradition of reading at the Jewish feast of Seder as a fulfillment of the ancient law in the Torah. The belief is that every Jew must tell his son the story of the centuries-old liberation of the Jews from Egyptian slavery.

The mural is a colorful story of slavery, deliverance and redemption. And, like the Haggadah, Shahn's mural in Roosevelt was created in three specific main panels.

The first panel tells the story of the arrival of Jewish immigrants from Germany and Eastern Europe and their struggles as they passed through Ellis Island and saw the Statue of Liberty for the first time. The second panel depicts what happened after they arrived, the immigrants' work in sweatshops in New York and living in crowded tenements, as well as the formation of their involvement in the labor union movement. The third panel shows success, the improvement in working and living conditions and the planning and development of their new hometown, a rural area complete with a factory, farms, a school and the people who made it all happen.

Shahn included in his mural likenesses of people he knew or who were involved in the immigration of the 1920s and 1930s. His own mother is shown as an immigrant arriving at Ellis Island in the first panel, together with Albert Einstein, a friend of Shahn's, and Raphael Soyer, a well-known Russian-born activist best remembered for his rallying against the fate of women in New York factories and sweatshops.

In the second panel, a crowd is gathered in front of the Triangle Shirtwaist factory, where the doors were locked to prevent union leaders from talking to the female workers. When a massive fire broke out in the wooden building, the women, trapped in the inferno, burned to death at their workbenches. The panel shows a union leader addressing the crowd and a placard with words by union leader John L. Lewis. The person depicted appears to be a composite of Lewis and David Dubinsky, the leader who headed the International Ladies' Garment Workers' Union. Local residents Shahn got to know in the Monmouth County community also appear in the crowd.

The third panel depicts some of the men who were responsible for establishing the Jersey Homesteads and features journalist Heywood Broun, New Deal advisor Rexford Guy Tugwell, New York senator Robert Wagner (the primary author of the National Labor Relations Act) and Sidney Hillman, who cofounded the American Labor Party the year before the painting was completed. Also shown in the painting, though only from the back, is Alfred Kastner, the innovative architect who designed the town with its unique geometric forms, flat-roof homes, communal areas and lush green land surrounding the community. Also shown is John Brophy, the first national director of the Congress of Industrial Organizations (CIO).

Shahn and his wife, Bernarda Brysen, did not leave Roosevelt once his work was complete. The couple had found hospitality, friendship and a rural environment in which they felt comfortable, and they decided to stay, at least for a short time. They never left.

That decision also gave the artist the opportunity to help out the town one more time.

Despite the efforts of the residents, an infusion of money from the government and supporters of the community style of life, Roosevelt began to fail, and morale fell as original settlers lost their investments and disagreement among local governing-body members impacted grants and loans from the government. But Shahn's presence brought an influx of artists and writers, and the community became known as a colony for culture and the arts. New residents also included pianists, opera singers and writers.

Shahn died in 1969 and is buried at Roosevelt Cemetery. His painting remains vibrant and vivid and is a stark reminder of what an earlier generation endured and overcame to start life in a new country.

—From *Atlantic Highlands Journal*, July 9, 2018

Congressman, Militiaman, Physician

By Muriel J. Smith

Even before the American Revolution, the name Scudder was highly revered and respected throughout the eastern part of the land that would become the United States of America, though there are varying accounts of when the Scudders first arrived and from which part of the British Isles they emigrated.

What is certain is that two Scudder brothers arrived on these shores in the seventeenth century, landing in Massachusetts, where one settled, while the other moved to Long Island and was well established there by 1630. That brother, Thomas, was a miller in Huntington, Long Island, married and had a son named Jacob. Jacob grew up on the island until he moved to what became known as Scudder's Mills, just southeast of Princeton, New Jersey. He and his wife, Abia, later settled near Monmouth Court House, a name used to describe the county seat at Freehold, where they raised their three sons and three daughters. Nathaniel was the eldest of the half-dozen children and was born on May 10, 1733, most likely at Freehold, although historians disagree about whether he was born there or on Long Island.

Nathaniel was in the fourth graduating class of the College of New Jersey, now known as Princeton, in 1751, and immediately launched into the study of medicine. During his years as a physician, Nathaniel was highly regarded and respected and had an extensive practice throughout the Monmouth County area. Early accounts describe him as enjoying "the respect and confidence of the people of that part of the State on account of his varied learning, strong powers of mind, genial disposition and purity of life."

Nathaniel married Isabella Anderson, the only daughter of Colonel Kenneth Anderson, the year after his college graduation and following a charming and whirlwind romance. The book *History of NJ Medicine* records the courtship and romance as told a century later by Dr. Scudder's granddaughter, Maria.

Seems that the beautiful Isabella, a member of an old Scottish family that came to the colonies during the Scottish troubles of 1715, came to church services on horseback and was quickly seen and appreciated by young college graduate Nathaniel Scudder. She alighted from her horse and fastened it to a tree before walking into the church. The daring young medical student went up to the horse, disarranged the equipment and entangled the bridle before he, too, went into church. When the service was over and young Isabella went back to her horse, only to be chagrined by the entanglement, Nathaniel suddenly appeared, quite dignified and graceful, and offered to come to her assistance. He righted all the reins he had entangled, then assisted the young lady as she got into the saddle. He mentioned to her that since they were both traveling in the same direction, a distance of some four miles or more, he felt the need to travel with her and offer her protection. She acquiesced to his gallantry, Nathaniel mounted his own horse and the two rode off

The crucial Revolutionary War battle fought in June 1778 near today's Freehold was called the Battle of Monmouth Court House. *McKay Imaging Photography.*

together, beginning a courtship that culminated in a marriage in 1752 and, ultimately, the birth of three sons and two daughters.

The young Dr. Scudder had a lucrative and popular medical practice in Monmouth County but also displayed his strong belief in a free nation separated from ties to England, as well as his belief in a strong religious foundation. He was a member of Old Tennent Church, where he apparently challenged Thomas Paine, of *Common Sense* fame, on a religious matter. Scudder bested the gifted New Englander in the verbal controversy.

As the colonies grew closer to war and New Jerseyans heard reports of British soldiers taking over and burning Boston, Dr. Scudder was among the first to become involved. At a meeting of citizens held in Freehold on June 6, 1774, a full two years before the Declaration of Independence, Dr. Scudder took a leading role and drafted resolutions of sympathy for Boston and support for the cause of freedom.

His involvement in the freedom cause came quickly after that, and he was named to numerous positions of authority and leadership. He became a member of the local committee of public safety, then a delegate to New Jersey's first provincial congress, which met in New Brunswick. He became speaker of the legislature within two years, and when the first Monmouth County regiment of militia needed more men, Nathaniel hung up his stethoscope and signed up. He became a lieutenant colonel in the First Regiment of Monmouth militia under Colonel George Taylor, whose father, Edward Taylor, owned Marlpit Hall.

By November 1776, five months after the Declaration of Independence was signed, Lieutenant Colonel Scudder was promoted to colonel and took charge of the regiment, the soldiers of which came from the Freehold and Middletown areas. Taylor had resigned his post to join the Loyalists.

It was neither glorious nor safe to be a rebel anywhere on the continent, but particularly in New Jersey, which contained the highest concentration of Loyalists among all the colonies. Families were torn apart by differences of opinion about whether this far-flung child of England should remain loyal to the king, although they would be laden with heavy taxes and no representation in British government, or take on the world's strongest nation and fight for independence. Loyalists, some of whom remained soldiers simply to act as spies and report troop movements to the British generals, burned or otherwise destroyed the homes of their rebellious neighbors and former friends, took their cattle and destroyed their crops.

The rebels could not honorably call themselves an army. They had no uniforms, received little or no pay, left their own families and farms to take up the cause and were often armed only with makeshift weapons. But

Scudder, as others like him, saw it as a worthy and honorable cause and bore all the burdens of leading an upheaval never before known, all for the cause of freedom from British rule. There followed a period known as the Tory Ascendancy, and unfortunately, Scudder, in command of Monmouth Militia troops, had little success. The militia dissolved.

With no troops to command, Scudder attached himself to a Pennsylvania Continental regiment; some other troops also followed. Thus began a monthlong, highly successful action to put down the Ascendancy.

Within a few weeks, the Monmouth Militia was reconstituted and spent the next month encamped on the hills of Highlands, with a mission to guard Monmouth County against a British invasion by their troops stationed at Sandy Hook. But by February, Scudder's militia was involved in the Battle of Navesink, surprised by the British and falling to them with the loss of more than two dozen militiamen killed and another seventy captured.

Dr. Scudder resigned from the militia to devote more time to rising in the political field, where he felt he could do better as a legislator. In 1777, he was elected as a delegate to the Continental Congress but did not attend a session for nearly a year because of his militia obligations. Throughout his two one-year terms in Congress, Congressman Scudder also missed a number of other meetings because of his military duties; he was a member of the committee dealing with the quartermaster service, a position that required a considerable amount of personal travel time. He declined to accept a third term, indicating that the heavy burden that his time away from home placed on his modest estate in Freehold made the obligation too demanding.

Records show that, in actuality, Colonel Scudder was not even in the militia in June 1778. At the time of his 1777 resignation to focus on politics, he relinquished his post as colonel of the first regiment to Asher Holmes. As it happened, he was at home enjoying a congressional recess in the summer of 1778 when British general Charles Lee began his march through Monmouth County. Scudder decided to join the fray that was so close to home, an encounter that became known as the Battle of Monmouth—the battle historians later called a turning point of the war.

While the battle was never seen as a clear-cut victory for the rebels, the British fled Freehold under dark of night while General George Washington was preparing an early morning attack. Routing the British after Washington's stunning losses in New York gave those who yearned for freedom the boost in morale they needed to continue waging the war.

With his retirement from Congress in 1779, Scudder devoted his full time to his military duties. He also served on the New Jersey Council of Safety, where part of his obligations included fining or jailing captured Loyalists in the areas, Monmouth among them, where there were no courts. He also served as the county's representative to the Privy Council, the Upper House of the New Jersey legislature.

That he knew his life was constantly in danger as a soldier was best evidenced in a letter he wrote to his son Joseph in 1780. Joseph was a law student in Philadelphia, and the worried father expressed concern for his son's future. He signed it, "with every sincere wish and prayer for happiness both here and hereafter, your most affectionate and careful Father."

Ironically, Nathaniel Scudder—doctor, congressman, New Jersey assemblyman, local leader, soldier, Patriot—came through the war years unscathed…until 1781.

Still affiliated with his old friend from the Monmouth Militia, General David Forman, Scudder was assisting the general in repelling Loyalist raids on Bayshore lands. The pair had formed the Retaliators, a vigilante group of Patriots viewed as both illegal and dangerous who were known for taking strong actions against Loyalists and suspected Loyalists. When a party of refugees landed at Sandy Hook and made their way undiscovered to Colts Neck, where they took six prisoners, the alarm was sounded at Freehold, and Dr. Scudder responded. Knowing the direction the refugees would head, he told his family that a battle was "expected at Long Branch. I will go down and bind the wounds of the poor fellows."

With other Patriots from Freehold, Dr. Scudder took off in pursuit of the Loyalists in an effort to rescue the prisoners. Near Black's Point (now Rumson), Dr. Scudder and General Forman were standing on the riverbank talking when a shot was fired, aimed at Forman. But, as the general told it later, he had taken an involuntary step backward, describing it as "the most fortunate step of my life." The bullet that missed Forman struck and fatally injured Dr. Nathaniel Scudder. It was four days before the Battle of Yorktown and the surrender of the British to their American foes.

Colonel Scudder thus became a casualty of the war—the only member of the Continental Congress to serve with the militia and be killed by the enemy. He is buried in Old Tennent Church Cemetery in Manalapan. At the Freehold Borough Hall, the second-floor meeting room is dedicated as the Scudder Room, and a glass wall, designed by local interior designer Nelson Kuperberg, depicts Scudder's writings, a scene from the Battle of Monmouth and a map of the area.

—From the *Atlantic Highlands Herald*, June 2016

30

The Despoiler of Freehold

By Muriel J. Smith

According to a municipal court judge in Freehold, in 1919, Alonzo Thompson was "a natural born criminal." Judge Lawrence went on to describe the convicted burglar as the son of "hard working parents." But, he explained further, "Alonzo had certain tendencies inherited."

According to the *Freehold Transcript*, in January 1919, Alonzo was "the despoiler of Freehold" who would be serving "many moons" behind bars, enabling "Freehold to breathe easy again."

Apparently, Thompson had a long history of crime and escape, according to a number of newspaper articles about him. At one time, he had been sentenced to prison for some break-ins around Freehold. While in prison, he made friends with the chaplain, and the friendship led to him getting an early parole.

But Thompson apparently didn't mend his ways, as he got another six to fourteen years behind bars for a series of robberies in 1915. He was in prison for four years on those counts when he managed to escape and, according to the *Transcript*, headed to their newspaper office in Freehold, where he got in through a rear window, searched through desks and apparently left without taking anything, leaving the place in disarray.

During the next few weeks, Thompson, according to the *Transcript*, tried Millers' Bakery, entering through a cellar window but never managing to reach the first floor. He then raided a couple of iceboxes and took some "eatables" before trying his luck at on the flag shanties along the railroad tracks. He also entered Annie Arrowsmith's vacant house—she was known to spend her winters in warmer climes—and ransacked the home and a few other places in the neighborhood.

Nobody actually saw Thompson during these escapades, which were spread over several weeks while police continued their hunt for the prison escapee. Because he had not yet been captured, local folks were sure he was behind the series of illegal entries. Or, as the *Transcript* reporter wrote, "all of these visits have been credited in turn to Alonzo."

About one month after his escape from a prison road camp, Alonzo Thompson met his match in the fine citizens and law enforcers of Freehold.

Around midnight on a Wednesday night in January, a night watchman, William D. Lykes, was making his rounds, checking the rear side of stores on the north side of West Main Street. He found a couple of robes on the ground behind William S. Brown's clothing store and called for help in looking for the man they were sure was Alonzo Thompson. One of the new hunters spotted a ladder sticking out of an open window in Brown's store, and the shop's owner was called. The hunt then led to a transom on the roof, and Constables James Conway and Wilson Hankinson conducted further investigations. Apparently, a crowd had gathered on the street for the evening's entertainment, and someone down below spotted Thompson running across the roof, away from the constables, and heading to the Trust Company building. In the meantime, two more constables, Hulse and Mulholland, were just about on the roof, having gone through a transom in the Burtis building. Someone spotted Thompson crouched behind a wall. "Constable Conway sprang upon the fugitive, and, finding Alonzo willing to put up a fight, he handed his rubber club to Mr. Hankinson with instructions to quiet the prisoner." The story concludes that "a tap on Alonzo's head had the desired effect and he was handcuffed and led to jail."

Constables found a fully loaded .38-caliber revolver and "a lot of bullets" in Alonzo's pockets, a suit of clothes, an overcoat and some ties from William Brown's stock, along with a six-dollar pair of gloves and other "loot." Police also took a gold thimble from Thompson's pocket that was inscribed with the initials "A.C.A."—unquestionably, they reasoned, the property of Annie Arrowsmith.

Three months later, Alonzo Thompson pleaded guilty to five incidents of break-ins and was sentenced to another twenty to thirty-five years of hard labor. He would have been sixty-nine years old when released if he served his full sentence.

—From the *Freehold Transcript*, January 3, 2019

31

THE MOLLY PITCHER OF CARLISLE

By Muriel J. Smith

I t's only a three-hour car trip along beautiful roads, but for historians who like to expand their knowledge of people whose names became known through Monmouth County connections, Carlisle, Pennsylvania, is a neat little community with pleasant people, lots of great restaurants and charming B&Bs that charge reasonable prices.

Carlisle, located in Cumberland County about twenty miles west of Harrisburg, the capital of Pennsylvania, dates to the 1700s, when John Armstrong laid out a plan for the city to accommodate the Scots-Irish who settled in the area to farm the land. Carlisle is about five miles in area, with just under twenty thousand residents, and is named for its sister city, which is also located in Cumberland...England.

For Monmouth Countians, probably the most famous name associated with Carlisle is Molly Pitcher, the camp follower who, legend tells us, carried water for the cannons and soldiers in the midst of battle and took her husband's place as a gunner when he was injured during the Battle of Monmouth, the turning point of the Revolutionary War.

This Molly Pitcher, Mary Hayes McCauley, died in Carlisle in 1832 and is buried in the local cemetery, her monument large and imposing, complete with cannon and American flag, and surrounded by fencing. The town, and Cumberland County, are justifiably proud of their connections to American history, and today, the city's businesses take advantage of it.

Almost adjacent to the cemetery is the Molly Pitcher Brewery, where any number of brews with fascinating names such as Cannonball Kolsch, Redcoat,

Patriot Pale Ale, Black Powder Stout and The Minuteman remind visitors of Molly Pitcher's days of fame. There's also the 1794 Whiskey Rebellion restaurant, highlighting the day when President George Washington led his troops to quash the insurrection of farmers from Pennsylvania and New Jersey who objected to the whiskey tax. The rebels left before any encounter with the troops, but the tax was not repealed until Thomas Jefferson became president.

Every Wednesday through December, there's also a terrific farmer's market set up in the heart of town, where one can purchase numerous products from the Amish, like pickled beets and coleslaw, along with great cheeses; other booths offer unique items, including alpaca fur products, salmon from Alaska and fresh produce. It's also a great area for wineries, and the Castleriff in the heart of town offers daily wine tastings and great company.

The city is also home to Dickinson College, named by Benjamin Rush after the Pennsylvania delegate to the Continental Congress who declined to sign the Declaration of Independence. President James Buchanan, the nation's only bachelor president, is also an alumnus of Dickinson despite almost being kicked out for bad behavior before being given a second chance at finishing his education.

Carlisle's Molly Pitcher—and locals are quite certain she is the Molly Pitcher of Battle of Monmouth fame—lies in the Old Public Graveyard, the resting place of no fewer than fifty-three officially listed veterans of the Revolutionary War, although research points to that figure being closer to ninety-five veterans. The larger-than-life statue atop the grave was not erected until the State of Pennsylvania commissioned it in 1916. Swiss sculptor J. Otto Schweizer, better known for his numerous sculptures, bas-reliefs and other works depicting the Civil War and its generals, designed the statue depicting a forceful Molly Pitcher who stands over the grave of Mary Hays McCauley. The stone itself, which now identifies the burial site, was placed and dedicated on July 4, 1876, fifty-four years after the death of Mary McCauley. The staff for the American flag, and the cannon also at the site, were not added until 1916, a full ninety-four years after her death.

Carlisle historical documents point to Mary Ludwig being born in New Jersey, near Trenton, on October 13, 1744. The daughter of a German-born farmer, she was raised on hard work and learned to be self-sufficient before she accepted an offer to move to Carlisle, where she joined the employ of the Irvine family as a housemaid; the head of the house, Dr. William Irvine, was a prominent physician in the town.

During her time there, she met William Casper Hays, whom she married on July 24, 1769. Hays was a barber and a Patriot, and he enlisted in Thomas

Mary McCauley or Mary Hays, a.k.a. Molly Pitcher, is buried in Carlisle, Pennsylvania. *Muriel J. Smith.*

Proctor's Artillery as a gunner in May 1777. As was common in the era, like many other wives, Mary accompanied her husband in the battle march, providing numerous services ranging from laundry and cooking to cannon-cleaning and tending horses and wagons for the military throughout the war. History shows that William Hays was indeed present at the Battle of Monmouth in late June 1778, and, presumably, his wife was still with him. Records indicate she was with him through the winter at Valley Forge just six months earlier.

With no records to prove otherwise, it is legend that Molly Pitcher—or anyone else, actually—took up the gunnery position for Hays when he was injured or felled by the intense heat and bright sun under which the Battle of Monmouth was fought.

After the war, Hays was issued two hundred acres of bounty land in Pennsylvania, and the couple settled on Lot No. 257 in Carlisle, where the veteran resumed his tonsorial business. It is also recorded that Mary Hays, a persistent woman, continued to beseech the government for a pension of her own, and in 1822, the Pennsylvania legislature awarded her forty dollars per year under "an act for Mary Ludwig Hays McCauley for her bravery during the Revolutionary War."

The couple had a son, Johannes Ludwig Hays, born in 1783; Mary's husband died in Carlisle in 1786.

Sometime within the next fifteen years, Mary married again, this time to John McCauley, a war veteran who had also been a friend of her late husband. Records show that sometime before 1810, the family faced hard times, and Mary was forced to sell, for thirty dollars, the original land bounty William Hays had earned. No records indicate any connection with McCauley after that time, but there are records of Mary Hays McCauley carrying on alone, making her own living tending to the sick and cleaning courthouses and other public buildings for the state of Pennsylvania. At the time of her death, on January 22, 1832, she was living at her son's home at North and Bedford Streets in Carlisle. She was seventy-nine years old.

Her gravestone reads:

> *Mollie McCauley. Renowned in History as Molly Pitcher, the heroine of Monmouth.*
> *Died Jan. 1832. Aged 79 Years.*
> *Erected by the Citizens of Cumberland County. July 4th, 1876.*

—From the *Atlantic Highlands Herald*, July 2, 2018

32

Does the Story of Molly Pitcher Hold Water?

By Rick Geffken

Every schoolkid in New Jersey learns that a young woman called Molly brought pitchers of cool well water to George Washington's troops during the Battle of Monmouth in June 1778. On that horribly hot summer afternoon when her husband fell, exhausted, wounded or dead, brave Molly took his place, loading and firing his cannon against the British. Did a real woman inspire this stirring story, or is it totally apocryphal?

John Fabiano, executive director of the Monmouth County Historical Commission as of 2019, introduced his Molly Pitcher candidate on Tuesday evening, October 24, 2013, before a crowd of about fifty people. "Local Origins of the Molly Pitcher Legend" was sponsored by the Township of Ocean Historical Museum. Basing his presentation on nearly twenty years of independent research, Fabiano made his case for Mary Hanna, an Allentown servant girl, as the model for Molly Pitcher. And, perhaps more surprisingly, he thinks she was also an intelligence agent for none other than George Washington.

Women in the Revolutionary War played important—if unheralded— roles as nurses, cooks and military aides. Twentieth-century historians thought Molly Pitcher was Mary Ludwig Hays, wife of a John Hays, who collapsed from heat exhaustion during the battle. Others posited she was Margaret Corbin, disguised as a man and fighting in the same regiment as Mary Hays. Or she could have been Deborah Sampson, who also wore a man's uniform and later received a federal pension for military service. A consensus evolved that Molly Pitcher was a conflation of these women—and probably others.

A nineteenth-century Currier and Ives lithograph of Molly Pitcher, which influenced the arguments, included this amateurish verse about "The Women of '76":

> *Her husband falls—she sheds no ill-timed tear*
> *The foe press on, she checks their mad career,*
> *But firm resolve—she fills his fatal post.*
> *Who can avenge like her a husband's ghost?*

Fabiano's interest in the legend began when his friend and Allentown neighbor Ann Garrison partnered with him on the 225th anniversary of the battle with the Friends of Monmouth Battlefield group and on the Road to Monmouth project in 2003. For Fabiano, all roads led to solving the mystery of Molly Pitcher.

Fabiano immersed himself in Revolutionary-era documents in various archives and libraries during his tenure as president of the Allentown–Upper Freehold Historical Society. Allentown came up so often in his readings that he eventually wrote a one-hundred-page paper on it and distributed it to other historical societies. Fabiano believes that Allentown played a larger role in the Battle of Monmouth than was previously recognized. On their way across New Jersey to Sandy Hook and eventually New York, the British army temporarily occupied the small western Monmouth County town. George Washington's targeting of the fleeing redcoats resulted in the Battle of Monmouth, which was fought across the fields and streams in today's Manalapan.

Though respected Monmouth County scholars like Samuel Stelle Smith and James S. Brown had pursued the Molly Pitcher legend to no avail, Fabiano wasn't discouraged. His years working in the finance offices of the State of New Jersey incline him to value details and proof—and persistence.

Reviewing a long trail of documents—letters, muster rolls and pension records—with the audience, Fabiano connected the dots to the obscure Mary Hanna, wife of John Cavanaugh, who served with the New Jersey Continentals. He believes she overheard valuable military information when she worked in the home of a Loyalist and relayed it to Washington. In effect, she was a spy. Fabiano's "aha" moment came when he found a receipt showing a cash payment from Washington's staff to a servant he believes was Hanna.

During the discussion following Fabiano's talk, several people asked skeptical questions about his linking of Hanna to the Molly Pitcher legend. They asked about the proof that Mary Hanna was actually on the field of battle with her husband. Fabiano replied, "My intent was to determine if my thesis would be considered plausible when presented to an objective audience, one not biased due to local pride [e.g., Allentown–Upper Freehold]. I welcome and anticipate these questions, which mimic my own."

Even if the inspirational Molly Pitcher legend is never verified, Fabiano concluded, "The overall story is so interesting that it could form the basis of a fictional novel about Molly Pitcher, perhaps titled *A Servant Girl at Mrs. Watkins*."

—From the *Howell Times*, August 2013

PART V: ALONG THE SHORE

33

CHURCH OF THE (SEVEN) PRESIDENTS

By Rick Geffken

Ninety-five years after Woodrow Wilson last vacationed in Long Branch, the little chapel where he and six of his presidential predecessors attended services is finally being restored from its sadly deteriorated state. St. James Chapel, known as the Church of the Presidents, was built on Ocean Avenue in 1879 and was home to the Long Branch Historical Museum Association for the second half of the twentieth century. However, age and the effects of ocean weather took a harsh toll on the historic structure.

James Foley, president of the museum association, spoke about the current restoration plans at the 117th annual meeting of the Monmouth County Historical Association (MCHA) on Tuesday, January 19, 2016, in Red Bank's Two River Theater. Foley noted, "There are many worthwhile local historic causes. But people forget the significance of this building—at least seven United States presidents visited Long Branch. This restoration project is a great opportunity to build on something truly historic that's right in our own backyard."

Foley acknowledged the advice of Monmouth County historian Randy Gabrielan, who praised the local group's work to date while encouraging the trustees to contact national donors who might underwrite the restoration of such a nationally significant building.

When Long Branch was one of the premier vacation spots in nineteenth-century America, Ulysses S. Grant was the first president to visit the famed Jersey Shore. Rutherford Hayes, James Garfield, Chester Arthur, Benjamin

Harrison, William McKinley and Wilson each attended Sunday services at the small church during summer respites from the White House. The chapel was built as a branch of the larger St. James Episcopal Church, also in Long Branch.

U.S. presidents were not the only famous visitors to America's seaside resort. "Beginning in the 1880s, wealthy families like the Goulds, Vanderbilts, Sloans and Drexels built elegant summer 'cottages' in nearby Elberon," Foley said. Then, as now, rich industrialists attracted politicians and vice versa.

The Long Branch Historical Museum Association took control of St. James Chapel when the Episcopal diocese deconsecrated the church and planned to raze it in 1953. The Church of the Presidents was eventually listed in the National Register of Historic Places in 1976, but inadequate funding delayed major repairs. The museum closed in 1999.

Foley became president around the time the museum shut its doors, and—with the approval of the board of trustees—put a plan in place to save it. Thanks to several substantial private donations, the old structure was stabilized—a concrete foundation was poured, and steel girders

The Church of the Presidents was built as St. James Chapel in 1879 in the Elberon section of Long Branch. *Library of Congress.*

were installed. Recently, $70,000 went toward painting, roofing and the reinstallation of the original stained-glass windows in the crenelated tower of the church. Foley said the yearly budget for the museum association is $100,000, which he hopes can be matched by federal, state and/or county grants. Besides financing, Foley said, "The association is looking for volunteers of any kind. We would love donated goods, services, researchers. Whatever your passion is, we'll put you to work."

Foley expects the museum to reopen in the next few years. Visitors to the 1260 Ocean Avenue location will see an assortment of presidential artifacts, including, notably, the U.S. flag that draped President Garfield's coffin in 1881 after his doctors could not save him during his Long Branch recuperation from an assassin's bullet. Foley also envisions the museum serving as a community center for various local groups.

"The association's mission is to interpret our historic artifacts by telling the story of the people of Monmouth County through our exhibitions and shows," MCHA president Linda W. Bricker said at the meeting on Tuesday night. She also announced that 2015 was the association's best year ever.

Two of the most successful events sponsored by the MCHA in 2015 were a Fourth of July public reading of the Declaration of Independence at its Allen House in Shrewsbury and the very popular exhibit at the Freehold headquarters building showcasing African American music and entitled "Spirituals to Soul." MCHA director Evelyn Murphy reported: "The three major themes for the MCHA going forward are collaboration with the community, self-assessment—moving from good to great—and advocacy."

Anyone wishing to join the Long Branch Historical Museum Association can visit their website or Facebook page: www.churchofthepresidents.org or facebook.com/ChurchOfThePresidents. For information about the Monmouth County Historical Association, visit www.monmouthhistory.org or facebook.com/monmouthhistory.

—From the *Two River Times*, January 21, 2016

34

The *Malta*: New Jersey's Largest Shipwreck Artifact

By Rick Geffken

For many years, a metal "flagpole" at the southwest corner of Ocean and Eighth Avenues in Belmar has towered above any other object along the seaside community's oceanfront. Anchored in concrete, the "flagpole" hoists no flag and contains no plaque to commemorate its placement. So, why is it there, and what is it? Let's examine the history of Belmar for clues.

In 1872, this small seaside community was formed as the Borough of Ocean Beach. A group of businessmen saw the advantages of luring summer guests to the lovely area bounded by the Atlantic Ocean, the Shark River and Lake Como. Its alluring beaches and refreshing breezes were among its chief attractions. The Ocean Beach Commission drew up a charter, bought the land and parceled it into lots for summer homes. Guests from northern New Jersey and New York immediately fell in love with the town.

By 1885, the commission had decided to change the borough's name, possibly to avoid confusion with other summer resorts with similar names. Avon, Wallmere, Malta, Elbro, Stratford and Shade were the suggested names. *Malta* was the name of a ship that wrecked off the Belmar coast that year. In 1889, the commissioners decided on the "City of Elco." The name lasted only a month, and Belmar became the official name on May 14 of that year.

The *Malta* was a full-rigged iron vessel sailing from Antwerp to New York when high winds and angry seas forced it aground at the foot of Ninth Avenue at Ocean Beach on November 24, 1885. It was stranded at 3:30

a.m., 250 yards from shore, during a furious gale and rainstorm. The surf was high and dangerous, and because it was a period of spring tides, the waves dashed well up on the beach and, in places, almost covered it. The *Malta*'s iron mainmast went over the side soon after it struck ground. As the heavy sea caused the ship to pound heavily on the bar, the shocks snapped it in two places, and the upper part fell overboard. The mizzenmast fell into the sea soon after.

The crew of Shark River Station No. 7 of the U.S. Life-Saving Service, the precursor to the Coast Guard, responded, and they were soon joined by members from the Spring Lake and Squan Beach Stations. After two failed attempts, they finally secured a line over the ship's rail to the foremast. The two-hour operation rescued all but one of the ship's twenty-four sailors by using the breeches buoy device invented by Joseph Francis of Toms River. The sailor who died jumped overboard in a panic and was carried away while he was trying to swim to shore. The ship was a total loss of nearly $76,000, though parts of it were salvaged over the next month. The remains of the hull were left in place and continued to deteriorate over the years.

The iron-hulled ship *Malta* came ashore at Ocean Beach (now Belmar) on November 24, 1885. *Belmar Historical Society.*

The proximity of the wreck to the "flagpole" on Eighth Avenue made me think there might be a connection between the two. Obviously, there is no one alive today who can remember the grounding of the *Malta*. Nor is there anything on the "flagpole" that identifies it.

I began with this: Why would the founding fathers consider naming the town after a shipwreck? Certainly, the remains of the *Malta* must have been a tourist attraction, which brought new visitors to the borough. Besides the tourist dollars they spent, some of them must have rented or purchased summer homes. It seems logical that Ocean Beach would want to keep that interest and connection alive. The problem was that as the wreck was being salvaged, it was slowly but surely disappearing. Someone might have had the bright idea to take the remaining mast from the ship and mount it on shore, close to the wreck. This would mark the spot for tourists to visit the site and also serve as a permanent memorial to the disastrous event. Naming the town after the ship would further strengthen Ocean Beach's claim to fame.

But is the "flagpole" actually the mast of the *Malta*? I think a case can be made by carefully comparing the pictures of the wreck with the "flagpole" as it stands today.

First, is the "flagpole" actually a mast? Several items identify it as such. At its bottom, there is a metal fitting, which is a shaffle. On wooden masts, shaffles were metal sleeves that helped secure booms to masts. The holes in the shaffle are called gudgeons (or braces). Pintles, or long hooks that were part of a gooseneck, fell into the gudgeons. On this "flagpole," the shaffle has been welded to the shaft.

Second, at the very top of this "flagpole" is a cap. Caps were fittings at the head or top of a mast through which an upper or topmast travels. The upper ring is the cap; the lower ring is a yoke or lower cap. The fitting on our "flagpole" is likely the upper cap. There would be no reason to have a cap on an ordinary flagpole.

Last, a metal rail runs almost the full length of the "flagpole." This rail would be used to help guide a sail up the length of the mast. It is likely that fasteners of some kind attached to this guide rail from the luff edge of the sail. These were pulled by sheets (ropes) through a block (pulley) at the cap and hoisted and lowered the sail along the mast.

Older ships with wooden masts used oak or metal hoops to run up and down the mast as the sail is hoisted or lowered. With a metal mast, these hoops would have created friction and noise and would have worn out much faster. The introduction of metal masts on sailing ships was probably accompanied by innovations like this guide rail.

This "flagpole" rail runs only partway up the mast and appears to stop four or five feet below the cap, about where a trestletree and a crosstree would be. So, it seems certain that our "flagpole" is indeed a mast from a metal sailing ship. But what ship?

The picture of the iron-hulled *Malta* on the beach clearly shows that the foremast survived the grounding. Intriguingly, the picture also reveals a cap at the top of the mast and a crosstree several feet below the cap, about where the rail stopped. The original photograph of the wreck appears to show a rail running along the front of the mast and what appears to be a fastener still attached to the rail. The proportions of the two masts seem to closely match. Though the mast on Ocean Avenue seems to be taller than the one in the wreck picture, that is an illusion, since the mast was stepped inside the hull of the ship on the keel; therefore, a good portion of it is out of the camera's view. We know from the Life-Saving Service report that the *Malta* had iron masts, and the mast on Ocean Avenue is iron. The *Malta* grounded at Ninth Avenue, and the mast is mounted at Eighth Avenue. There are no other obvious shipwreck candidates. All the pieces seem to fit. The unmarked and unidentified "flagpole" in Belmar is, in all probability, the original foremast of the wrecked *Malta*.

—From the New Jersey Historical Divers Association's *Journal*, Vol. 6, No. 1, 2002

Note: In August 2018, Dan Lieb, president of the New Jersey Historical Divers Association, wrote to Rick Geffken: "BTW: four copies [of this Malta article] were given to Belmar; one for the historical society, one for their record, a backup copy, and one for Mayor Pringle. As you may know, the mast was salvaged and used as a vent for the boardwalk septic system [hence the pumphouse nearby]. He said he received his copies days after I dropped it off at Borough Hall. He had come from a meeting where they discussed tearing it down as an eyesore but was now going to save it as a historic site, which he did. He even had a special plaque mounted at its base. Furthermore, he and his son learned to scuba dive at [your old store] Divers Two just so they could visit [the shipwreck remains]."

35

The Jersey Skiff, the King Family and Goldie

By Muriel J. Smith

The Jersey Skiff has often been called the "sports car of the water"—it is easily recognized and highly touted as a Jersey Shore invention and the most famous of all the different boats built along the coast. Highlands' own Stewart King was one of the original builders of the skiff back in the days when it was a wooden lapstrake construction with oak ribs all riveted together. King had more than two hundred patents for skiff designs based on the vessels he and his family built at the King Boat Works on South Bay Avenue.

But the King men weren't the only famed King family members in Highlands. No one who went to school here in the 1950s and 1960s could forget Goldie, the matriarch of the twentieth-century clan.

Goldie Viola Bogue was a native of Highlands, a loving mother and a no-nonsense woman with a big heart and a stern voice that gained immediate attention. She was also the lady who checked on kids' attendance in school; at the local public school, Goldie was the truant officer, and at Henry Hudson, she was the attendance officer.

Goldie was a woman who loved her hometown—she loved it so much, in fact, that she always used to say she just couldn't get away. In actuality, she did get away; she and her husband, George (also a native of the borough and the son of the original Sea Skiff builder who continued the family business through his and the next generation), loved to travel. Goldie boasted that she visited every one of the forty-eight states of her time except Oregon. And

The very first Jersey Speed Skiff was built by Oceanport's Pappy Seaman in 1922; he named it *PJ. Ned Lloyd*.

she's never found anything better than Highlands, she'd say, adding, "and I don't suspect Oregon's any nicer than any other place."

As the truant officer at the elementary school, Goldie got the list of all the children who were absent from school each day, then either telephoned their homes or stopped by and made a visit to find out why. She'd forgive late arrivals, knowing the children probably were sent on their way to walk up the hill on time but dawdled along the way. Kids of that age didn't really resort to playing hooky too much, she'd say, either because they just weren't that adventurous or were afraid of the consequences. It was an era when chicken pox, mumps, measles and the like were common and ran rampant through a classroom. Goldie knew which disease was running at any particular time, but she still made those phone calls or visits just to be sure.

It was a different story at Henry Hudson, where the teens were a lot more adventurous and knew when the fish were running or when a few had something special planned. It was an era, she once explained in an interview, when "the parents expected the children to do their share, and the children just don't sometimes, especially when working parents had to leave home earlier in the morning than the students." Some parents would really be surprised, she said, when she alerted them to the truancy; others didn't seem to mind too much.

Although there's no doubt that just about every Highlands school-age youngster of the 1950s and 1960s knew Goldie King, there were many more who knew her because of her involvement in numerous community activities. She was a virtual pillar of the Methodist church, where she was the organist, and active in the church's Golden Circle ladies' group. She was also an avid bowler and active in the PTA and many civic organizations.

At home, Goldie and George raised seven children, and their offspring continued the King tradition of working hard, doing good for others and reminding everyone that Highlands was the best place in the world to live.

—From the *Atlantic Highlands Herald*, July 17, 2017

36

The William Sandlass Family

By Rick Geffken

"I mmigrants," Lin-Manuel Miranda sings, "get the job done." Monmouth County Genealogy Society (MCGS) members are testimony to the truth that the daughters and sons of immigrants get jobs done, too. A family of German and Irish immigrants who came to Monmouth County in the mid-nineteenth century illustrates extraordinary industriousness.

When twenty-five-year-old Johann Wilhelm Sandlass arrived on our shores from Dorndorf, Germany, he was willing to work hard to create a more prosperous life for himself. The young carpenter moved to Shrewsbury in York County, Pennsylvania, where he and his wife, Anna Elizabeth Herman (1832–1918), started a family. Their offspring eventually included two girls (Lena, b. 1861; and Elizabeth, b. 1870) and five boys (Louis August, b. 1855; Oscar, b. 1857; Frederick William, b. 1862; Charles, b. 1864; and Andrew, b. 1866). Johann Sandlass, called John in his new country, eventually relocated to Baltimore County in Maryland, where he died in 1897. Anna outlived him by another twenty-one years.

Of all their children, it was Frederick who may have made the greatest mark. Assimilating quickly into American culture, he was known as William. He followed his father into the carpentry trade for a bit and then recognized the opportunities for advancement and new careers in New York City. By the early 1880s, he was a wholesale spirits salesman in and around Manhattan. He serviced customers near Coney Island, which was then becoming the famous American playground on the southern shore of Brooklyn.

His timing was fortuitous. Coney Island had become a fashionable beach resort after the Civil War, with some reports claiming that twenty-five to thirty thousand people visited on summer weekends during the 1880s. Railroad lines and steamboat ocean piers were built to bring ever increasing numbers of vacationers to "the best beach on the Atlantic Coast."

Entrepreneurs were eager to amuse these people, if not to help them spend their money. LaMarcus Thompson, considered by some to be the father of modern roller coasters, put up a Switchback Gravity Railway at Coney Island in 1884. As the name suggests, passengers sat in cars propelled down parallel tracks by gravity from one "station" to another and back at the astonishing speed of six miles per hour. The ride's popularity inspired a wide variety of other entertainments, such as dime museums, concert halls, dance pavilions, sideshows, circuses, fireworks displays, games of chance and an aquarium. The model for the modern amusement resort was established.

Young William Sandlass Jr., observing all of this, was inspired. He had a contact—a successful New York banker named Ferdinand Fish—who bought some Jersey Shore land as part of a group named the Highland Beach Improvement Association. As part of the firm's plan to sell building lots for seaside cottages in what would become Sea Bright, Fish needed a way to attract potential buyers. Sandlass had just such an idea—put up a thrill ride.

Sandlass signed a lease for four acres between the Shrewsbury River and the Atlantic Ocean. In 1889, the Great Switchback Rail Road, another ride designed by Thompson, was the first thing he put up at what he called the Highland Beach Excursion Resort. The Great Switchback Rail Road was the most prominent building along the northern Jersey coastline next to the Twin Lights, which was built on nearby Mount Mitchill in the Highlands in 1862. Sandlass began to advertise, targeting day trippers from New York City and northern New Jersey.

People from all over flocked to Highland Beach. Fish sold plots of land for cottages to the south of the resort. Sandlass opened a second building, a bathing pavilion, to attract bigger crowds. With five years of its construction, the Switchback Gravity Railway was surpassed by faster rides elsewhere. Sandlass, always quick to adapt to the changing leisure market of the emerging American middle class, built a family home from the timbers of the old roller coaster. The Sandlasses lived above the first-floor grocery store. The house became the headquarters of the rapidly growing entertainment complex on Sandy Hook.

William Sandlass Jr. constructed his Great Switchback Rail Road, a prototypal roller coaster, on Sandy Hook in 1889. *Susan Sandlass Gardiner.*

Within ten years, crowds of over ten thousand people per day were visiting Highland Beach's bathhouses, merry-go-round, Bamboo Garden, Surf House Restaurant and Hotel, ice cream and soda stores and the Mel-Rah Club. The club, with its clever backward spelling, was a jazz venue that featured New York bands. Beaches on the Shrewsbury River and Atlantic Ocean side of the narrow resort offered summer guests a prime escape from the heat and humidity of the cities. Sandlass even rented blue woolen bathing suits for those without them.

Highland Beach was renamed Sandlass Baths around the time its founder died (in 1938) and was hugely successful for its lifespan of seventy-five years on the Jersey Shore. Part of that success was due to the thirty-three extended Sandlass family members who lived and worked at Highland Beach.

William's widowed mother, Anna (1832–1918), was integral to the operation until she passed away in 1918. His brother Andrew (1866–1948) and sister Elizabeth (1870–1959) worked at the business almost every summer. Until her death after a tropical cruise in 1908, William Sandlass's first wife, Catherine (b. 1861, née Mattingley), was at her husband's side as he grew his business. Her sister Margaret Mattingley was happy to help. William and Catherine's son William Thomas (1886–1966) no doubt thought Highland Beach was his personal summer playground when he was a boy. His first wife was Ariel B. Cashion (1884–after 1938).

The immediate Sandlass family lived in the 1893 house, but as the resort grew, other members of the extended clan were housed in the Surf House Hotel or even in the upstairs rooms of various bathing pavilions and other buildings. William Sandlass generously employed as many family members as he could to fill the roles of ticket-takers, servers, lifeguards, washers, sweepers, car-parkers, cleaners, cooks and probably bottle-washers, too.

Four years after his first wife died, William Sandlass married New Yorker Helen Lynch (1885–1969). She immediately immersed herself in the Highland Beach operations and was a vital part of them with their son, Henry (1913–1969), after William died. For a time, Helen's mother, Bridget (née Farley, 1862–1940), born in Ballieborough, Ireland, worked at the resort. A cousin of Helen's, Bernie Lynch (1860–1931) was another Irishman glad to find work among family in his adopted country.

Mae Lynch Smith (1888–1961), sister of Helen, was the first of fifteen Smiths and their in-laws who worked for William Sandlass at various times over five decades at Highland Beach.

Henry Sandlass's wife, Irene "Midge" Sheehan (1918–1970), happily raised five children in the old Sandlass home at the foot of the Highlands–Sea Bright Bridge until 1962, when Sandlass Baths finally closed. That was the last year for Sandlass Baths, because the State of New Jersey took the property under eminent domain in order to build up Sandy Hook State Park.

Henry and Midge's children were Susan (b. 1944), Irene "Duffy" (1945–2014), Helen Ann (b. 1946), Hank (b. 1947) and Sheila (b. 1951). William Sandlass's granddaughter Susan Sandlass Gardiner has worked to preserve her abandoned family home on Sandy Hook for the last ten years. She was the prime mover behind the establishment of the nonprofit Jersey Coast Heritage Museum at Sandlass House, which was disbanded in 2019 after almost three years of ultimately unsuccessful efforts to save the old Sandlass home.

—From the *Monmouth Connection*, January 2017

37

Christmas and Ice on the Shrewsbury

By Muriel J. Smith

An old upright piano and her grandmother playing her old favorites inspired a young lady from Sea Bright to learn to play the piano. As a teenager, Susan Sandlass took piano lessons for two years because she loved the strains of "Smoke Gets in Your Eyes" and "Jeanie with the Light Brown Hair" that filled the air when she and her siblings arrived home from school as their grandma serenaded them with music.

Or maybe it was the Christmases in the 1940s and 1950s, when the Shrewsbury River was almost frozen all the way from Sandlass Beach to Bahrs Landing Restaurant in Highlands; it was too dangerous to ice skate there, so families chose the safety of nearby McCarter's Pond in Rumson or the edge of the river just off Wardell Avenue in Rumson.

Or maybe it was the old Victrola, with Bing Crosby crooning out "White Christmas" from those 78 rpm records, or Perry Como's Christmas medley that could melt the hardest of ices or hearts. These were the favorites of the other grandmother who also filled an entire family with love and happy memories; Helen Sandlass was the matriarch who—with her husband, William—continued work at the summer resort, Sandlass Baths, late in the nineteenth century after William's first wife, Catherine, died; he and Helen married in 1912. It was their home on the beach where family and friends gathered, always knowing there would be laughter, music and love.

Whatever the reason, the winter season, especially the Christmas season, was a most happy event around the Sandlass home at the north end of Sea Bright.

Henry Sandlass Sr. with his children (*from left*) Ann, Sheila and Hank on a frozen Shrewsbury River during the winter of 1957–58. *Susan Sandlass Gardiner.*

Usually, weeks before the holiday, the children all gathered for their traditional hunt for the gifts they knew they could expect. Their parents always hid the presents around the house, and Susan and her four siblings would go on a surreptitious hunt to find them. It was a big part of the excitement.

Susan Gardiner remembers it well. She's one of the five Sandlass children brought up in the big house amid a loving three generations of family who loved the clamor, noise and excitement of summers filled with visitors and vacationers but cherished the warmth of the big fireplace in the living room and the magic of family celebrating the holiday together during the wintertime.

The piano stood in the foyer, and it was Grandma Sheehan who especially brought it to life and gave Susan the yearning to play just like her. And it was Grandma Sheehan's sister, Susan's great-aunt Ella, who was the star of the show at Christmas dinner. Aunt Ella was the baker in the family, and the entire family waited all year for her dessert buffet filled with pies and cakes she spent days making. There were always four choices of pie—mince, apple, pecan and lemon meringue—plus two traditional cakes, chocolate and coconut. The kids began getting hungry for them as soon as all the aromas emanating from the ovens in the kitchen wafted through the air.

But desserts had to wait. First, there was the grand Christmas dinner. That was always prepared by Mae Heineck, a cook extraordinaire, who arrived from her home in Highlands early in the morning to prepare the family's huge feast before heading back home to enjoy the day with her own family.

The kids never did learn where their Christmas tree came from. It just seemed to appear, magically, on Christmas Eve, brought in by their dad, Henry Sandlass, to be decorated with homemade and family-saved ornaments. It had its own place of honor in the big house—right in the corner of the living room next to the porch door. It always had to be tall enough to brush the ceiling with its highest branches and was filled with silver tinsel. Grandma Sandlass would have her favorite carols playing on the Victrola as everyone joined in to decorate the tree before the young ones were whisked off to bed in anticipation of an exciting Christmas morning.

Christmas Day meant that the Sandlass House would be filled with relatives and friends sitting around a roaring fire in the large fieldstone fireplace in the living room. For the festive dinner, the dining room table was always set with a large snowman as the centerpiece and four smaller snowmen on the table.

Susan Sandlass and her siblings gathered in Grandma Sandlass's room first thing upon waking. Helen Sandlass always had a small tree under her bay window upstairs, and the first gifts opened were always the ones from her that could be found under that tree. Then, everyone headed downstairs for more love and laughter, the gifts beneath the family tree in the living room, a bedlam of joy and excitement that only increased as cousins, aunts and uncles began arriving for the daylong celebration.

They had their own gifts to give, too. The children saved money during the year so they could go out together a few days before Christmas to buy presents for their parents and grandparents.

The years when the river was partially frozen are the ones the kids remember the best. It would be filled with huge chunks of ice, chunks that moved very slowly down the river, under the bridge, and continued on their way to the Navesink or returned on the outward tide to head toward the tip of Sandy Hook. In spite of yearnings to hopscotch on the icy pieces across the river to Highlands, there were always the warnings to stay off the chunks, which, to youngsters, looked like magnificent ice floes.

As recently as 2016, that upright piano was still in the Sandlass House at the eastern edge of Gateway National Recreation Area at Sandy Hook. The National Park Service recently reported there are no immediate plans or funds for the building's demolition; Congressman Frank Pallone met with the leaders of former nonprofit Jersey Coast Heritage Museum at Sandlass

House and dashed off a letter to the National Park Service in support of saving the building. However, by 2019, despite the efforts of historians, family members and interested local residents, it appeared that all efforts to preserve the Sandlass House were futile.

And the piano? It's now in the corner of the family room—the only piece of furniture left from the Sandlass era. If you listen carefully, it's probably got some stories of its own to tell.

—From the *Atlantic Highlands Journal*, November 29, 2016

38

THE GREATEST UNKNOWN JERSEY SHORE BEACH RESORT

By Rick Geffken

Destinations Past: Highland Beach was voted "Best Home Grown Documentary Short—New Jersey History" at the 2017 Garden State Film Festival. Created by first-time filmmaker Chris Brenner, the short film played for enthusiastic Atlantic City crowds in April 2017. Brenner's movie tells the story of William Sandlass Jr. and the Highland Beach Excursion Resort he opened on a mostly remote Sandy Hook peninsula in 1888. It makes a convincing case that this day trippers' getaway was the north Jersey Shore's contribution to the changing recreational patterns of late-nineteenth-century Americans. It was the place that helped launch the Jersey Shore tourism business.

Brenner employs century-old color postcards and remarkably crisp black-and-white photographs, as well as home movies and family vacation snapshots. While these are common enough elements in historical documentaries, this thoughtful offering makes compelling use of them as it revisits an important time and an influential place overlooked by New Jersey historians.

The forty-two-minute production by the Fair Haven, New Jersey native reveals William Sandlass as one of the first people to understand and exploit the trend of short-term vacations that the fin-de-siècle middle class was starting to enjoy. Before Highland Beach's Victorian-style buildings were constructed, the more famous Jersey Shore resorts of Long Branch

Chris Brenner's (*center*) *Destinations Past: Highland Beach* won a "Best Home Grown Documentary Short—New Jersey History" award at the 2017 Garden State Film Festival. *Garden State Film Festival.*

and Atlantic City catered mostly to upper-class folks who would spend a week or so enjoying the amenities at those legendary resorts.

To entice working-class people with more limited means, Sandlass filled his resort with inexpensive amusements, like a merry-go-round, an ice cream and soda parlor, two music clubs, an Airdrome outdoor movie theater, a photo studio, bathing pavilions, bathhouses, a waterfront hotel and restaurant and an outdoor food-and-drink emporium. The Highland Beach Excursion Resort, nestled on a sandy fifty-yard strip between the Atlantic Ocean and the Shrewsbury River, was a natural draw for city dwellers. Huge crowds flocked to both the coastal and river beaches that Sandlass filled with boardwalks and pavilions. He built it, and come they did—sometimes twenty thousand people in one day.

The film's opening clip, of a Jersey Central Rail Road train chugging through Highland Beach ("All aboard!"), starts us on our journey. Photographs, maps and contemporary advertisements presented via the familiar Ken Burns pan-and-scan effect show the people, places and parties of a lively scene that spanned eight decades.

Destinations Past: Highland Beach's establishing shots position the resort as part of the post–Civil War, Industrial Revolution–era, changing American culture. Historical and contemporary aerial photographs of Sandy Hook immediately make clear why Sandlass's resort was advertised to Manhattanites as "the nearest available beach on the New Jersey Coast." Brenner uses a remarkable little film clip to illustrate Coney Island's influence on what Sandlass built at the Jersey Shore. Delightful frames from the famed Brooklyn amusement area show well-dressed riders on a "Gravity Rail Road," the same kind that propelled adventurous vacationers at "the reckless speed of 6 mph" at Highland Beach a few years later. LaMarcus Thompson, the father of modern roller coaster, designed both thrill rides. The Highland Beach version was put up in 1889, just five years after the one on Coney Island.

Absent from the film are the ubiquitous talking heads explaining the obvious, a frequently overused documentary technique. Brenner wisely chose to omit "experts" and simply allows contemporary images to guide us through the resort's history. This narrative flow acknowledges viewers' intelligence.

Destinations Past: Highland Beach makes ample use of German lithography postcards, prints from *Frank Leslie's Illustrated Newspaper* (the 1899 America's Cup race was held just off Highland Beach), glass plate photographs and old home movies and snapshots taken by Brenner's father, Ted, during the time he worked as a "Beach Patrol" boy and a bartender at the resort. The late Ted Brenner was the source for stories about the grand resort and the inspiration for his son's yearlong filmmaking project.

This film is all the more remarkable because Chris Brenner produced it himself while working as a traveling representative for a major technology company and participating in various civic organizations in Fair Haven, only a few miles from the former site of Highland Beach. Brenner may be a novice filmmaker, but this debut is as good as many professional documentaries.

A brief clip from director D.W. Griffith's 1910 film *The Unchanging Sea*, starring a very young Mary Pickford, looks like Sandlass's bathhouses, although film historians now agree it was actually shot on the California coast. Regardless, Griffith shot at least four films in and around Highland Beach (including 1909's *Lines of White on a Sullen Sea*). The fledgling American film industry began in Fort Lee, New Jersey. The Highland Beach resort was used more than once for location shots.

Brenner's understated voiceover narration helps us understand the unique story of a carefree retreat that has but a single remnant—William Sandlass's house. Speaking with the ease of someone who knows his subject well, Brenner employs the conversational style of one old friend talking to another about the good old days.

The film's soundtrack features period-correct, old-timey music (such as the perfect 1902 song "In the Good Old Summer Time"), jazz and ragtime standards (such as those by Scott Joplin) and 1940s hits (such as those by Duke Ellington and the Andrew Sisters). Viewers are sweetly seduced by the gaiety of Highland Beach and mesmerized by the tumultuous times through which it endured—the Great War, the Jazz Age, Prohibition, the Depression, World War II, the Eisenhower postwar years and, finally, the early 1960s. The evocative soundtrack enhances the rarely seen images, providing vital context for the seventy-five-year run of the Highland Beach resort.

Highland Beach was more than a popular diversion from summer heat and humidity. New Jersey's public officials had to rethink transportation infrastructure near it to accommodate the thousands of visitors. The Central Railroad of New Jersey, in response to the overwhelming number of people heading south from New York to the Jersey Shore, abandoned its long-used ferry terminals on Sandy Hook and built a new pier in Atlantic Highlands. The so-called crisscross bridge of 1892 connected those rail lines to Highland Beach as it crossed the Shrewsbury River. New Jersey State Highway 36 was constructed to help funnel automobile traffic over the 1932 "Million-Dollar Bridge," the successor to the crisscross bridge.

Brenner's wonderful little film is on line at www.destinationspast.com or via YouTube (search for "Highland Beach"). Take the time to view Brenner's newest effort, his documentary called *Rumson Hill*, about the Gilded Age McCarter family estate. More stellar work is sure to come from Chris Brenner's Navesink Studios.

—From *New Jersey Studies: An Interdisciplinary Journal*, Summer 2017

PART VI: ALL AROUND THE COUNTY

39

What's in a Name? Mystery and History in Farmingdale

By Rick Geffken

Today's independent Borough of Farmingdale was part of Howell Township until 1903. Even today, many people think of it as just another section of Howell, like Ardena or West Farms. But aside from its separate identity, how the name of this little town evolved is an intriguing story in itself.

It's no surprise to most local residents that the Borough of Farmingdale changed its name from the less prosaic Upper Squankum around 1854, possibly as early as 1846. Even further back in time, the original name of the small village was Marsh's Bog. Many people may assume that peculiar name was a somewhat reluctant tribute to the indigenous wetlands that were ideal for cranberry bogs. Just a few years ago, the Manasquan River Watershed Association put up signs labeled "Marsh Bog Brook" along one boundary of the town. The real surprise is that the soggy topography is not the source of this name, either. So where did the names "Marsh's Bog" and "Upper Squankum" originate?

English Quakers William Reape and his wife, Sarah, first settled in the Rhode Island Colony. William frequently sailed on business between Newport and Gravesend, Long Island, in the 1660s. When he died in 1670, he had never occupied New Jersey lands he owned—and may not have ever visited them.

By 1685, William's widow, Sarah Reape, was living on a large plantation on the Shrewsbury River. She eventually accumulated over two thousand

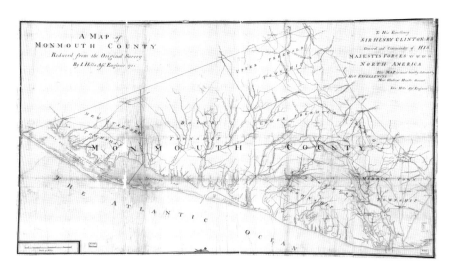

John Hills created this Monmouth County map for the British general Sir Henry Clinton during the Revolutionary War. *Library of Congress.*

additional acres in Monmouth County, including tracts near the current location of Farmingdale. When her daughter, also named Sarah, married a Rhode Island merchant and maritime trader, the young couple realized that they, too, had the opportunity to get rich by investing in land. Among the many parcels they bought, one was described in their property deed as

> *All that tract of land and meadow situate in Monmouth County heretofore purchased of ye Indian owners and Proprietors of ye same under their hands and seales, beginning at the westerly end of Job Throckmorton's land upon the Manasquan River, commonly called and known by the name of Squanacoung.*

The Lenape name Squanacoung meant something like "the place of entrance to the river." The white settlers of the area heard it as Squanacome. Spelling in those days was often subject to whims. Many early deeds show variations like Squancum and Squancome, but eventually Squankum became the standard. Later still, locals differentiated Lower Squankum from the place a few miles north, Upper Squankum.

The younger Sarah Reape's husband was a Rhode Island businessman named Jonathan Marsh. He was interested in extracting iron from the abundant streams and bogs. He bought as much land containing flowing water as he could afford, most of it straddling a certain brook he thought promising. In the summer of 1701, wanting to consolidate his holdings, he purchased one more piece of property described as "a tract lying on the west side of said Jonathan Marsh's bogg on a brook that runs into Manasquan River." And there, we have the very first description of what is now the western boundary of Farmingdale—Marsh's Bog Brook. Over time, as a few simple houses were built in the pinelands around that brook, the little settlement took its name from Jonathan Marsh. It was called Marsh's Bog before it was anything else.

The Goodenough House in Farmingdale was originally located at the corner of the main road from Squankum and the road to Shrewsbury/Tinton Falls at the southwest corner of a one-hundred-acre tract of farmland. Although local lore dates the house to 1690, the Goodenough family did not own it until 1822. The house is frame-built with architectural characteristics of both Dutch American– and English cottage–type dwellings. Monmouth County houses built before 1850 were frequently composites of several styles and types rather than "pure" examples. Common Dutch American homes were made of wood and clad in shingles or clapboard, with a one-room plan—a rectangle of squat, squarish proportions. English cottages were one and a half stories, one room deep, also of heavy timber fame construction.

The Goodenough House was expanded at least twice—the earliest two sections formed the eastern part, and a taller and final addition formed the western part. This second addition is in the Greek Revival style popular between 1830 and 1840. The original living section, measuring about twelve by twenty-three feet, has the most rudimentary construction. Besides hand-hewn timbers, this section also has Dutch Colonial elements like a hearth fireplace on the middle of one sidewall, a door next to the fireplace leading to tight-winder stairs and walls lined with handmade bricks. The house originally had a dirt floor, with wide planking added later.

Land ownership records and historic wills indicate that the sisters Isabella and Graham Kearney inherited the one-hundred-acre tract in Marsh's Bog from their maternal grandmother, Isabella Graham Morris, in 1752. Isabella Graham Morris was the wife of the first colonial governor of New Jersey, Lewis Morris, who served from 1738 to 1746. Both of the granddaughter heirs were unmarried at the time—Isabella was thirty-six, and Graham was only nineteen.

Graham Kearney married Reverend Samuel Cooke in November 1756, and they settled near Shrewsbury Town, close to his Christ Church headquarters. The still-single Isabella decided to oversee their joint property in Marsh's Bog. She either moved into a house previously built by a caretaker or hired someone to build a rudimentary dwelling for her. Baptismal records from Christ Church indicate that she owned several slaves who also may have helped her build it.

A 1763 deed notes that there was property "south to the highway that goes from the Falls to where Ezebel Carneys [*sic*] now lives." This highway is now Asbury Avenue, then called the Road to Tinton Falls.

When Graham Kearney Cooke died in 1771, the property passed to Samuel Cooke but was still co-owned by his sister-in-law Isabella. With seven young children to care for in addition to his missionary work, Cooke turned to her for help. No doubt, this is when Isabella expanded her small home to three rooms and one and a half stories.

The home and property passed through several owners after 1779. Eventually, Joseph Goodenough bought a two-acre corner lot and the house in 1822. Active in community life, he served as a justice of the peace and postmaster and was a member of the Freehold Circuit Court. He and his wife, Hannah, had five living children by 1831, and not long afterward, he put the final addition on the old house.

The Wainright House in Farmingdale was built between 1739 and 1749 by Joseph Lippincott. *Rick Geffken.*

The home remained in the hands of Goodenough descendants until 1956. It was moved to Goodenough Road, just a few hundred yards away, the following year.

However, the oldest house in Farmingdale is probably the Wainright House at 48 Main Street. The first Wainright (sometimes spelled Wainwright) to own this house was Halsted H. Wainwright II, who bought it in 1831. His father, Halsted Wainwright I (1771–1818), rented the house to run a business with a post office as early as 1817, when it was owned by the Corlies family. While it became locally known as the Wainright House, does it actually date from an earlier time, and if so, who built it?

Britton Corlies bought 207 acres of a 345-acre tract from the Robert Lippincott estate in 1793. The land belonged to Corlies, and then his son David, until 1823. And though we know that David Corlies operated a sawmill at the southern end of the pond behind the house where he lived, earlier owners likely built the original structure.

The Proprietors of East New Jersey sold 345 acres of a large Marsh's Bog tract to Stephen West in 1690. The proprietors' deed specifically states that the acreage was "bounded, abutted by barren lands unsurveyed"—meaning that no one was living in the vicinity at that time. West was a Massachusetts Bay Colony planter and land speculator who never moved to New Jersey. In 1739, West sold the property to "Joseph Lippincott, yeoman." A yeoman was a working farmer who owned his own land but still depended on his neighbors to exchange necessities like other foodstuffs, tools, candles and clothing.

Joseph Lippincott's son Robert was twenty-six when he married Rebecca Tilton in 1749 and probably moved his young bride into his father's house. Two years later, Joseph Lippincott's will was witnessed by Adam Brewer and other neighbors who definitely lived nearby, providing circumstantial evidence that Joseph did in fact live in a house on this property.

All the historical documentation, together with the house's architectural characteristics, suggest that the Wainwright house was built by the Lippincotts between 1739 and 1793, most likely within ten years of 1750.

—From the *Howell Patch*, May 2013

40

How Howell Township Came to Be

By Rick Geffken

Richard Howell was born in Newark, Delaware, in 1754. Raised a Quaker (the Society of Friends), he married another Friend, Keziah Burr, the sister of Aaron Burr. Howell was a lawyer and a soldier in the early U.S. Army, serving as a major of the Second New Jersey Regiment. He participated in the crucial battles of Brandywine, Germantown and Monmouth. He spent the winter of 1777–78 at Valley Forge with George Washington and the beleaguered Continental army.

After serving on the New Jersey Supreme Court, Richard Howell became New Jersey's governor in 1793. He ran virtually unopposed for six consecutive terms. New Jersey's constitution made the governor the commander of the militia; President George Washington ordered Howell to lead the state militia into Pennsylvania in 1794 to crush the Whiskey Rebellion. Farmers there were resisting a new tax on the whiskey made from their leftover grain and corn. Howell's popularity with voters, and his participation in the Battle of Monmouth, gained him notoriety. Howell Township was incorporated by an act of the New Jersey legislature on February 23, 1801.

At the end of Howell's last term as governor, Republican opponents accused him of failing to account for all the funds for military preparedness. Under this cloud, Howell died in Trenton in April 1802. Despite the Quaker emphasis on peace, Howell's war experiences led him to become an Episcopalian. Ironically, this enthusiastic military man is buried in that city's Friends Burying Ground.

Howell's early roads, originally Lenape Indian trails, connected many of its farms with the Manasquan, Metedeconk and Shark Rivers for transportation of crops, as well as for trade with other farms, gristmills and sawmills. Major roadways would eventually be incorporated into Route 9 and Route 33. Other highways were named for their connections between locales: Lakewood-Farmingdale Road and Ramtown-Greenville Road. Still others were named for their ultimate destinations (Georgia Tavern Road) or functions (Stagecoach Road, commemorating the 1850s stagecoach service along Route 524).

As the more northern sections of Monmouth County filled with towns and villages during the nineteenth century, Howell stayed considerably rural, with abundant farmlands and diverse crops. The many waterways lent themselves for use as cranberry bogs throughout the area. By the 1870s, almost 170 acres of cranberries had been planted in the township.

By the early to mid-1800s, the population in and around Howell Township had grown significantly, and many schools and churches were built to accommodate the growing population. The Methodist Church Society, founded in the 1760s, was one of the first in Howell. The very first Methodist meetings in Monmouth County were held in a Howell barn. The Bethesda Methodist Church at Adelphia was built in 1779.

Over the years, portions of Howell Township were taken to form Brick Township, Wall Township, Farmingdale and Lakewood. Within the township, suburban neighborhoods developed: Adelphia, Bethel, Fairfield, Jerseyville, Ramtown, Squankum, New Bargain, Fort Plains and Freewood Acres.

Bethel, in the southwest part of Howell, was settled in 1865, when Israel Reynolds donated a lot for a Methodist church, which was completed a year later. A schoolhouse, store and post office were all in place by 1882. The area's name was eventually changed from Bethel to Southard.

First used by local farmers, the natural fertilizer called marl was discovered around 1830 during the construction of a dam for Henry Clayton's gristmill in New Bargaintown. Soon, it was being exported to New York and other markets in the northeast. The unearthing of local marl had a major impact on the growth of a particular little village section in Howell.

The village known as Marsh's Bog became Upper Squankum in 1815, then Farmingdale in 1854. Its local marl pits brought prosperity in the form of entrepreneurs, tourists and the attendant businesses. Like few other parts of Howell, Farmingdale became a center of commerce in the nineteenth century and was home to churches, taverns, shops and other establishments— so much so that it separated as an independent borough in 1903.

Religious groups settling in Howell included Jewish populations, Buddhist Kalmyks and Russian Orthodox communities.

Howell became home to businesses as diverse as a drumhead factory, blasting powder manufacturers and brickyards; these businesses included Rogers & Co. drum head factory, Phoenix Powder Manufacturing Company and both the Lippincott and Brocklebank brickyards.

Historic Howell continues to offer a mix of rural and urban life in the twenty-first century. Modern schools and shopping centers are close to farms with grazing cattle, horses and cornfields. Newer homes are neighbors to houses built before the Civil War. Contemporary houses of worship are located just down the road from the clapboard spires of traditional Christian churches.

—From the *Howell Times*, August 2013

41

ADMIRAL EARLE AND THE
NORTH ATLANTIC MINE BARRAGE

By Muriel J. Smith

Naval Weapons Station Earle, formerly Earle Ammunition Depot, in Colts Neck was named for a retired admiral who was unique, formidable and a hero of World War I when he served as chief of the Bureau of Ordnance and earned a reputation as an expert on guns and explosives.

Vice Admiral Ralph Earle was born in Worcester, Massachusetts, in May 1874 and graduated from the Naval Academy in 1896, the year before the United States entered the Spanish-American War.

He served in that war and on several different ships, including the USS *Missouri*, the second ship of its class named for the Show Me State, showing his heroic stance when there was a tragic disaster aboard the battleship.

Earle was aboard the *Missouri* at the time of a disastrous turret explosion, and his actions earned him commendations from President Theodore Roosevelt; later, he would receive praise and support from the assistant secretary of the navy who later became President Franklin Roosevelt, fifth cousin to Theodore.

The *Missouri* was commissioned in 1904 and, during sea trials off the coast of Virginia the following year, had an accident made less ruinous only by the quick actions of Earle and others in the crew. During gunnery training, the port twelve-inch gun in the rear turret flared backward, firing at and igniting three charges in the turret, starting a fire that took the lives of thirty-six men. However, action by other sailors and officers prevented the fire from spreading to the magazines and saved the ship. Several officers, including Earle, were honored for their actions.

It was during his term as chief of the Ordnance Bureau that Earle achieved his greatest accomplishment—designing and promoting a plan that was rejected, at first, by all except then–assistant secretary of the navy Franklin Roosevelt. The North Sea Mine Barrage challenged every other leader who said it was too dangerous and could never be accomplished. Today, it is regarded as one of the navy's greatest achievements during the First World War.

Earle's plan was to blockade the route German U-boats took to reach areas they were patrolling in the North Atlantic. It called for laying a minefield in the North Sea with a new type of mine, the Mark VI, which he described in his letter to Chief of Naval Operations Admiral William Benson as "having been tested with excellent results." His idea called for planting 72,000 mines filled with

Ralph Earle, an 1896 U.S. Naval Academy graduate, was the World War I hero for whom Naval Weapons Station Earle in Colts Neck is named. *U.S. Department of the Navy.*

22 million pounds of molten TNT to create 300 miles of barriers for the U-boats; keeping another 100,000 mines for replacements (if necessary) and another 25,000 for the U.S. coast, all at a cost of $40 million. The North Sea emplacement would cover a length of 230 miles and be 15 to 35 miles wide.

The mines would be built within three months, at a rate of one thousand per day, at St. Julien's Creek depot in Virginia, and the entire matter had to be conducted in complete secrecy; "advance information of such a mine would be of the greatest aid to the enemy in devising means to counteract it," Earle told Benson. Earle also pointed out that liners and merchantmen, together with destroyers and light cruisers, would be necessary to carry out the mission in the short time frame he projected, and "the whole barrier should be laid as one operation."

The success of the operation would mean almost certain destruction of the U-boats, which, at this point, had sunk more than 800,000 tons of food and supplies being shipped to England. The German naval leaders were predicting that their U-boats' success was leading to a victory over England, since it made it possible for the enemy to sink British vessels faster than they could be replaced.

The Royal Navy was opposed to the North Sea Mine Barrage plan, thinking it was impracticable to carry out and could not be effective; Vice Admiral William S. Sims was also skeptical. Even navy secretary Josephus Daniels called the plan "a stupendous undertaking—perhaps not impossible but to my mind of doubtful practicability. The North Sea is too rough and will necessitate withdrawing all our ships from other work."

But Roosevelt, who knew of Earle's actions during the *Missouri* incident, was enthusiastic about its success, and with his support, the plan was finally approved by the Allied Naval Conference in September 1917. The following month, the mine-laying began, and it continued for a year in thirteen different excursions.

There is no official record of the number of U-boats that were blown up in the barrage, but what was evident was the large decrease in the number of attacks on Allied shipping vessels. The impact on the morale of U-boat crews was startling, however; many crews simply refused to leave their bases and patrol the North Sea. One U.S. admiral wrote that the mine field created panic among enemy crews in submarine flotillas. One captured U-boat commander called the mines the "most dreaded" of all Allied anti-submarine measures.

Although the barrage was initially opposed, and many were doubtful about the success of the mission, in the end, British rear admiral Lewis Clinton-Baker, who commanded the British force during the operation, described it as "the biggest mine planting stunt in the world's history."

Earle retired from the navy in 1925 after more than thirty years in the service. He then served as president of Worcester Polytechnic Institute for fourteen years, gaining a reputation (and the love of the institute's students) for implementing a five-year plan that led to a swimming pool, a new hall and other campus improvements. He died following a stroke on February 13, 1939. Two years later, the USS *Earle* was launched at the Boston Navy Yard, and two years after that, the Colts Neck ammunition base was opened and named for him to honor his association with many ordnance projects and ideas.

Admiral Earle is buried at the Quaker cemetery in Leicester, Massachusetts. His oldest son, Ralph Jr. (1900–2000), also graduated from the Naval Academy and also retired as a vice admiral; he is buried at the Naval Academy Cemetery in Annapolis, Maryland.

—From the *Atlantic Highlands Journal*, October 17, 2018

42

The 1944 Hurricane at NWS Earle

By Muriel J. Smith

The Great Atlantic Hurricane, the storm of September 1944, is still listed as one of the worst to ever hit the Jersey Shore. It was a memorable night for Lieutenant E.J. Benshimol, pier barracks duty officer during the 1700 to 2400 (5:00 p.m. to midnight) shift on September 15 at Naval Ammunition Depot Earle. The base at Colts Neck and its pier in Leonardo, connected by a road and a railroad, were less than a year old.

Through the official logs of the officer on duty at the pier barracks throughout the storm, you can almost feel the rising of the water, loss of power and bravery and camaraderie of the sailors and marines homeported at the Leonardo waterfront.

It was a Category 1 storm in the days prior to 1953, when the National Weather Service began to give hurricanes official names. It was also 1944—the nation was at war, and along the New Jersey coast, volunteers were patrolling beaches and the waterfront on regular schedules every night in search of any U-boats or other enemy intrusion on the East Coast.

Lieutenant Benshimol received his first call indicating the frightening night of duty he would be facing at 1800 (6:00 p.m.), an hour after he had relieved Lieutenant Miller as duty officer. The electrician notified him that all power on the piers was being shut off, but the pump house and barge pier power would remain. Lieutenant Benshimol alerted the fore company and the marines about the activity.

A half-hour later, the storm's intensity had increased so much that it prompted Benshimol to log "wind velocity increasing to almost hurricane proportions. Rain now a deluge." Fifteen minutes later, the lights in his office went out, the wind was increasing ("a continuous howl surrounds us") and the officer was keeping his log under the faint daylight that still remained.

Fifteen minutes later, it was reported that the walls of one of the buildings were saturated, and the roof was leaking. Benshimol instructed the sailors to keep the floors swabbed and try to stop the leaks. At their request, he also authorized that the heat be turned on.

Ten minutes later, a serious electrical problem, most likely from downed wires, was reported—there were no lights or power anywhere, and no fire alarm. Benshimol noted that the wind was "simply furious" and noted that with downed power lines, all would depend on telephones. Then he wrote, "May God sustain the telephone wires." He was now writing his log under a flashlight.

Officers from other locations on the base and at the pier were asking for work details to handle other problems that were rapidly cropping up; Benshimol issued the orders. He also gave one of his two flashlights to the storekeeper, who reported that the storeroom in the cellar was flooded, and he had gear to move; another pair of ordnance trainees reported in to help secure the locks on the doors of the freight cars on the navy rail line at the pier. The duty officer reported that it was 1940 (7:40 p.m.), and "waves are breaking over the outer end of the Pier."

The winds and rain increased, the calls kept coming in to the duty officer, sentries were posted for fire watch and the CO called to ensure everything possible was being done to protect the men and the pier. The team leader of the detail sent to seal the train doors called to report that they were stuck in the van, the water was rising and the bus couldn't make it through to give assistance.

Then, matters got worse, and Lieutenant Benshimol recorded his own actions and quick thinking: "Took fire truck (Chevrolet pick-up) all others being out of commission and went down toward the Pier....made our way with great difficulty...rain and wind absolutely impenetrable....Marine guards were evacuating vehicles. I was warned not to go down on the pier, water was up over it."

That was when Benshimol learned that "there were ten of our boys out on the Pier as pump watches...I came back to get permission to evacuate if it should seem necessary. After that I would go and get our men off the pier."

The official responses from Commander Tate, after consulting with Captain Green, were to not go out alone and not prepare the barracks for evacuation.

The next call came from sick bay—the door had blown off, and rain was coming in. Benshimol called for carpenters to go and repair the damage.

At 2140 (9:40 p.m.), the duty officer reported that the wind had abated somewhat, "though of course, not down," so he headed to the pier in a truck. He was only a half-mile out on the three-mile-long pier before the bay breaking over the truck forced him to return. The marine guard still on duty reported that there were "four of our boys in the pump house," and the train was coming to pick them up. Benshimol's driver was Seaman First Class Joe Evans, a sailor he praised for being "very skillful in avoiding objects on the tracks, planks, debris, manhole covers blown up and yawning holes. He avoided many a wave, too, that came dashing up at us."

The marine guard informed Benshimol that the train had evacuated the sailors. Barracks R13 reported eight of ten men in crew returned, and since the weather seemed slightly improved, Benshimol decided to send the fire chief and Evans, along with three of the sailors who had been in the detail, back to the pier in the belief the two missing men might be in the smoking house. They found that the men had taken refuge there, and Benshimol logged, "they are well, and happy to be back and safe." The fire chief reported, "the wind had shifted, and we shall very likely not have further difficulty. I believe I'll turn in."

The firehouse bell was being checked to ensure that it could sound an alarm in an emergency, Benshimol reported, after which he was turning in until 0600 reveille.

The following morning, September 16, 1944, Benshimol reported that a Coast Guard boat had run aground in Atlantic Highlands; seven men were injured, and all were in the hospital. In the chow hall, however, without power, no breakfast had been prepared, and hungry sailors and marines could look forward to a cold breakfast. When it was ready, it consisted of cereal, milk, bread, canned corned beef and fruit. The commissary steward reported that he'd try to wash dishes in cold water. The basement and boiler room were heavily flooded.

At 0800, Lieutenant E.J. Benshimol signed off of duty: "Relieved by Lt. Miller." It had been a busy night.

—Previously unpublished

43

GENERATIONS OF THE SWARTZ FAMILY SETTLED IN MONMOUTH

By Muriel J. Smith

There's never been any doubt that the Doctors Swartz—the father-and-son team of Dr. Harry and Dr. Steve—have been the favorite physicians of families in the Bayshore for many years. Both worked together for thirty-five years in the office Dr. Harry opened in 1956 on Cherry Tree Farm Road in Middletown. After Dr. Harry's retirement in June 2017, Dr. Steve moved his office to Palmer Avenue in Holmdel, where he carries on his dad's traditions at Mid-Atlantic Medical Associates and has gone on to garner many devoted and loving patients. Dr. Steve stepped down as medical director and head of the cardiac program at the Care One Care Center—where he had the reputation of being there, administering to residents, almost any time of the day or night—to devote more time to his new office. Dr. Steve is also the regional medical director for the Physicians' Practice Enhancement medical team in Shrewsbury.

The people of Highlands have a very special reason for being such admirers of this dynamic father-son team. It's not a very well-known fact among today's followers of the physicians, but their ancestors, who came from Russia, actually settled in Highlands, where one of them had a furniture store and grocery store, complete with ice cream. The family of Harry Swartz and his brother Lou Schwartz (they had different spellings of their surnames thanks to Ellis Island immigration officials) were part of the wave of Eastern European Jewish immigrants who helped settle their corner of New Jersey in the late 1880s.

Emanuel Swartz (*seated at lower left*) and his parents, Harry and Minnie Swartz (*far right*), outside the family's Swartz Variety Store on Bay Avenue in Highlands circa 1910. *Swartz family.*

To solidify that connection between the Old and New World, Dr. Harry's grandmother, Minerva, was a member of the famed Parker family, who are recognized as one of the first families in the community and the family for whom Highlands got its nickname of Parkertown.

The U.S. Census of 1900 tells the Parker story. This was the very first census taken in Highlands, since the borough had only come into its own a couple of months before. Until that time, Highlands (and Atlantic Highlands, up until 1887) was part of Middletown, which pretty well covered most of the waterfront in the Bayshore.

Back to the Parker family. There were only 848 people living in Highlands in 1900, as recorded in the census, with the population just about equally split between males and females. The 848 people made up 197 families, and 63 of those people answered to the name of Parker. Those 63 people lived in 16 different households, all with the name of Parker, representing more than 7 percent of the total population of Highlands in 1900.

One of those Parker women, Minerva—or Minnie, as she was known, was the daughter of William and Katherine Burdge Parker, but at that time, she did not answer to the name of Parker. That's because she was married to Harry A. Swartz, a well known and highly respected furniture and grocery store owner in Highlands. His businesses were located at the northeast corner of Bay Avenue and Miller Street.

Minnie and Harry had three sons and a daughter: Morris, Emanuel and Lavina all lived in Highlands, and Samuel lived in Red Bank. Their son Emanuel, born in Long Branch in 1902, is the father of today's Dr. Harry, who was obviously named for his grandfather. Emanuel was also the owner of the Swartz Furniture Store on Route 35 in Middletown in the 1930s and 1940s, and it was in the back of this store that Dr. Harry used to sit by the stove to study and do homework. Emanuel had special reasons to love Highlands. He met his bride, the former Dorothy Berkowitz, when she came by ferry to visit the summer vacationland of Highlands.

Harry Swartz, father of Emanuel and grandfather to Dr. Harry, died in 1929 at age seventy, according to his obituary in the *Asbury Park Press*, from a "complication of diseases."

Dr. Harry's grandmother Minnie outlived her husband for another eleven years, dying on December 29, 1940, in Middletown, where she had moved four years earlier. Her obituary said that she had been in failing health and under the care of a physician for several years and died of a sudden but fatal heart attack. At the time of her death, her daughter Lavina had moved to Shrewsbury, Samuel was still in Red Bank and Morris and Emanuel were living in Highlands.

Minnie's sister, Leola Parker Bush, and her brother, Forman Parker, survived her and still made their homes in Highlands. Both Minnie and Harry are buried at the Red Bank Hebrew Cemetery, in Lincroft, which is maintained by Congregation B'Nai Israel.

The Jewish Heritage Museum of Monmouth County in Freehold continues the story of the Lou Schwartz side of the immigrant family during the nineteenth century in Monmouth County.

Lou was a salesman in the Red Bank area, well known for his traveling horse and buggy and his vast supply of household items for sale, including everything from needed notions to the most desirable household items. After years working as a traveling salesman, Lou opened an antique store in Red Bank, got married and raised his family.

His son, Maurice, served in World War I with the U.S. Army. When he was discharged at the end of the war in 1919, he opened a truck and automobile showroom on Maple Avenue, which was, at that time, little more than a busy dirt road. Within two years, Lou moved from that location to West Front Street and continued what would become a landmark local business until the twenty-first century, when the automobile dealership was moved to Shrewsbury.

—From the *Atlantic Highlands Journal*, April 30, 2018

44

THE HOLMES-HENDRICKSON HOUSE

By Rick Geffken

I magine for a moment that Garret Hendrickson, who died in 1801, reappeared inside his still-extant farmhouse in Holmdel. Hendrickson would feel, well, right at home walking through the wood-frame house he bought from his cousin William Holmes in 1756. He'd recognize the Dutch floor plan, with two large front rooms and smaller rooms in the rear of the house. Glancing into the separate kitchen wing, he'd look for his slaves, who labored and lived there.

Once he stepped outside his brick-red–painted home, Hendrickson would quickly be disoriented. How on earth did his house wind up here, just down the road from his Longstreet relatives? What did the "Monmouth County Historical Association" sign in his front yard mean? What was that huge dark structure in the middle of the fields he used to plow? Wasn't that where his house should be?

What Hendrickson couldn't know in this imaginary scenario was that the Monmouth County Historical Association (MCHA) has restored and cared for the "Holmes-Hendrickson House" since 1959, when it was moved from its original location. After Bell Labs bought the old farm property in 1929, the engineering company needed room for a huge office building. Hendrickson's two-hundred-year-old house was moved to 62 Longstreet Road under the stewardship of the Freehold-based MCHA. After a careful and expensive restoration, the MCHA opened it to the public in 1965.

Now, the MCHA is pursuing a "use and occupancy agreement" for the Holmes-Hendrickson House with the Monmouth County Park System

(MCPS). As Chuck Jones, interim director of the MCHA in 2018 and 2019, explained: "Our goal as an organization is to be 'a shining light on the top of the hill' when it comes to preserving Monmouth County history. As we continue our work on a transformational strategic plan this spring, it was easy to identify that deepened relationships with other strong organizations like our park system were good for MCHA and even better for a property like Holmes-Hendrickson."

When the agreement is officially enacted, the Monmouth County Park System will provide ongoing maintenance at and improvements to the property. Jones emphasizes that the MCHA will continue to run its popular educational programs and provide docents for the Holmdel landmark. For instance, the popular Wool Days celebration at the Holmes-Hendrickson House took place on April 28, 2018, from 12:00 p.m. to 3:00 p.m. Activities included spinning and weaving demonstrations, indigo dyeing and perusing the craft fair, which featured a variety of local artisans. The event was free and open to the public.

Gail L. Hunton, chief of the Acquisition and Design Department of the MCPS, added: "The acquisition process is moving along but not finalized and has to be officially approved. MCPS purchased a conservation easement over the Holmes-Hendrickson House and property in 2011. We are pleased to be able to work with the historical association to permanently protect one of the most significant colonial Dutch houses in Monmouth County and New Jersey and look forward to their continued program use at the historic site after it becomes a park system property."

The Holmes-Hendrickson House was built by Garret Hendrickson's first cousin William Holmes in 1754. The house combined elements of both Dutch and English eighteenth-century architecture, befitting the heritage of the Hendrickson and Holmes families. These families, among the first to settle in and around Holmdel, were also among those who held the most slaves in Monmouth County. Garrett (an alternate spelling) Hendrickson himself signed a 1774 petition opposing the manumission of slaves—he needed them to work his vast acreage and support his twelve children by three successive wives: Catharine, Helena and Nelly.

George Beekman's 1901 *Early Dutch Settlers of Monmouth County, New Jersey*, notes that Hendrickson owned "some of the best farming lands in Monmouth County…well stocked with cattle, sheep, and swine." He grew crops, raised sheep for wool and planted flax to produce linen. His prosperous "Pleasant Valley" farm—and the farms of his neighbors—were frequent targets of British raiders throughout the Revolutionary War. While he was a lieutenant in the Monmouth Militia, Garret Hendrickson participated in several skirmishes against the British. He was wounded in 1780 and held prisoner for a brief time two years later.

Hendrickson survived the war and went back to work his farm. His descendants lived in the house until 1873. For the next fifty years, the house slowly deteriorated, until Bell Labs bought the property and moved the farmhouse to its current setting.

In 2018, the Holmes-Hendrickson House officially became part of the surrounding Holmdel Park, a natural fit. The park will eventually include trail connections with the Longstreet Farm and the other attractions in the verdant and popular public space.

Oh, and let's not leave a conjured Garret Hendrickson in front of his beloved house, dismayed and bewildered at the fate of his homestead in 2018. Rest in peace, Garret. Be assured that the very best Monmouth County organizations will care for your home and legacy for years to come.

—From the *Two River Times*, March 8, 2018

45

OCEANPORT: SURPRISING HISTORY AND A BRIGHT FUTURE

By Rick Geffken

Ask New Jerseyans about Oceanport, and most will mention Monmouth Park Racetrack or Fort Monmouth. But ask how the town on the South Shrewsbury River got its name, and even many of its six thousand residents might give you a quizzical look.

Luckily, Oceanport resident Frank Barricelli is busy researching the town he's loved since he began working as an engineer at Fort Monmouth in 1966. He's documenting Oceanport's historic connection to the Atlantic Ocean and aiming to finish a book in time for the 2020 centennial celebration of the borough's incorporation.

Oceanport was formed in April 1920 after cleaving itself off from Eatontown Township. Two hundred and fifty years earlier, Sarah Reape, the widow of one of the twelve Monmouth Patentees, William Reape, settled at Pumpkin Point there. She was the first known European settler on the neck of land called Port-au-Peck. Barricelli lives on the part of her former property now called Sands Point.

"The town's founding actually centered on today's Wharf Park area," Barricelli says. Charcoal and lumber were stored dockside before they were shipped to New York City through the Shrewsbury Inlet. The long–sanded-over inlet was opposite Black Point (Rumson) when Sandy Hook was still an island. "Known as the Eaton Town Dock, our town began as a seaport for much of this part of Monmouth County," continued Barricelli. "James P. Allaire built a wharf and warehouse here in the 1830s."

Wagons from Allaire's Iron Works in Howell transported manufactured ironware like pots and teakettles to the dock. Though the Manasquan Inlet was closer to his furnace and factories, Allaire chose to build at the Eaton Town Dock. County historian Randall Gabrielan explained: "The Manasquan River was probably a muddy stream in a sparsely settled region then, and, of course, one could not build a dock on the ocean," he said. "In addition, the open ocean voyage from there would have been that much longer."

Barricelli emphasizes that he is not the only one on the historical committee working on the book, just the primary researcher. "The idea for a new book actually came from the late mayor Maria Gatta. She gave me a copy of the 1970 'Oceanport in Retrospect' and asked me to update it. When she passed away, I lost interest in the project until two years ago." His enthusiasm was reignited when he joined the Environmental Restoration Advisory Board for Fort Monmouth.

Barricelli describes how the town's fortunes declined in the nineteenth century due to two impactful events. Though storms had closed and

Summer Meeting at Long Branch is a lithograph of the first Monmouth Park racetrack. *Library of Congress.*

The Signal Corps Camp, pictured between 1915 and 1920, evolved into the U.S. Army Signal Corps Headquarters at Fort Monmouth. *Library of Congress.*

reopened the Shrewsbury Inlet many times, it closed for good around 1845. Ships were forced to take the longer inside route up the Shrewsbury River and around Sandy Hook to get to New York. When the railroad pushed its way through the "Ocean Port" in 1861, the wharf business could no longer compete.

Oceanport experienced a business revival when Monmouth Park Racetrack opened in 1870; it was relocated west of the current track in 1890 and finally settled at its current location in 1946. It's now owned by the New Jersey Sports and Exposition Authority.

World War I also revived Oceanport when the U.S. Army built Camp Alfred Vail, renamed Fort Monmouth in 1925. About 30 percent of the now decommissioned U.S. Army Signal Corps headquarters is in Oceanport. The rest is in parts of Eatontown and Tinton Falls.

Oceanport's mayor John "Jay" Coffey sees both the racetrack and the former army base as vital to the town's future. "Just a few years ago, we were concerned with the viability of Monmouth Park Racetrack, Oceanport's largest employer and our largest tax ratable. Now, with legalized sports wagering in New Jersey, the better the track does, the better it is for Oceanport," said Coffey.

Coffey enthused about a recent visit to Monmouth Park. "On Father's Day, my wife and I stopped by the track for a few races. We heard all kinds of music all over the park. The great smell of hamburgers, hot dogs and horse poop permeated the air. Upwards of twenty-five thousand people were there. The vibe and electricity of life at the track is back!"

Coffey is proud that Oceanport paid $1 million for thirteen acres of Fort Monmouth property, allowing it to relocate its Oceanport Municipal Complex. "We won't have to put up anything new. We'll be rehabbing existing space—a courthouse, community center, DPW, town hall, a library, even a jail. We'll have it all done by September 2019. Oceanport is trending upwards."

—From the *Two River Times*, July 12, 2018

Philip Freneau: More Than a Poet

By Muriel J. Smith

He was a poet, a scholar, an editor, a politician, a farmer and a sea captain. He was a New Yorker who was educated at Princeton and later moved to Matawan. He roomed with James Madison at Princeton, and they remained close friends throughout their lives. He was also a friend of Aaron Burr, Henry "Light-Horse Harry" Lee and William Patterson, who later became governor of New Jersey. And both Matawan and Highlands are proud to include him among their finest friends of the Revolutionary era.

This was Philip Freneau, the "Poet of the Revolution." To many, he is the father of American literature.

Freneau was the oldest of five children, and it was his mother's wish that her firstborn would become a minister. With his brilliance and aptitude to learn, he was educated at home in theology and tutored under Monmouth County's learned William Tennett before he entered Princeton as a second-year student. Although drawn to the ministry, Freneau learned early that he was drawn more to literature. When the American Revolution broke out, he used his wit and literary ability to bring the era's politics into the poetic world and educate the people about the American Whig Society.

His style was eclectic, and he could write satire and comedy as well as patriotism and inspiration, be it for the Revolution or the sea, recalling the time he visited islands and wrote naval ballads.

His college years present several chapters of a fascinating and involved life on their own. Freneau had already been recognized as an accomplished

PHILIP FRENEAU
"The Poet of the Revolution"
1752 - 1832
Matawan, N. J. (Middletown Point)

Philip M. Freneau of Matawan was a renowned Revolutionary War poet. *Matawan Historical Society.*

poet from his writings about everyday life, nature and all that interested him. But the soon-to-be nation of the United States of America and the leaders urging revolution piqued his interest, as well, and he turned to political writing. Together with Madison and others, Freneau revived the Plain Dealing Club at Princeton and renamed it the American Whig Society, the oldest college literacy and debating club in the nation. The founders of the new debating club include many of the same names as those involved in the formation of the new nation—Princeton president John Witherspoon, later a signer of the Declaration of Independence; William Patterson, recognized as the prime mover of the American Whig Society; and William Livingston, a trustee of Princeton and, later, New Jersey's first governor.

It was obvious that Freneau reveled in the hotly contested debates between his Whig Society and Aaron Burr's Cliosophic Society, which was formed at Princeton around the same time. One example of this is something Freneau wrote (with another student), *Father Bombo's Pilgrimage to Mecca in Arabia*, a narrative of life in eighteenth-century America. That work, owned by Princeton, is considered to be the first work of prose fiction in the United States, and it earned Freneau the title of "Father of American Literature."

Freneau also wrote, with Hugh Breckenridge, "The Rising Glory of America," a patriotic poem that predicted a unified nation stretching from the Atlantic to the Pacific Ocean.

In spite of his reputation and accomplishments at college, it was during the years leading up to the Revolution that Freneau, prodded by Madison (who saw the strength of Freneau's writing and the impact it would have on those urging separation from England), was in his prime. He had already decided against a career in education and turned to journalism, becoming an editor in New York.

Freneau was thirty-eight years old and a seasoned sea captain—and accomplished in many other areas, as well—before he married Eleanor Forman and turned away from the sea to devote his time to writing and farming. Both his former college roommate and Thomas Jefferson urged him to start his own paper; this became the *National Gazette*, which he published in Philadelphia as a strong and fervent supporter of Jefferson's beliefs, in opposition to papers that favored Alexander Hamilton. Later, he served for a brief time as a clerk in Jefferson's White House, working with foreign languages for the secretary of state. It won him the praise of Jefferson, who said that Freneau's writing "saved our Constitution which was galloping fast into monarchy," and the distain and criticism of George Washington, who referred to him as "that rascal Freneau."

For the last thirty years of his life, Freneau worked his farm in New Jersey and occasionally returned to the sea as a trader. But he spent most of that era writing poems and essays and leading verbal attacks against corruption. As his funds dwindled, he sold off small portions of his estate.

While many consider "The Indian Burying Ground" his greatest poem, Monmouth County looks toward Freneau's "Neversink" as one of his best. The poem states: "These heights, the pride of all the coast," and "Proud heights! with pain so often seen/With joy beheld once more," and calls them "retirement's blest abode."

The Poet of the Revolution died in Matawan in 1832, two weeks short of his eighty-first birthday, and is buried at Mount Pleasant Cemetery in Matawan. The pyramid tombstone recalls his "upright and benevolent character." It is inscribed: "Heaven lifts its everlasting portal high and bids the pure in heart behold their God."

—From the *Atlantic Highlands Herald*, March 18, 1917

47

WHO WAS RED BANK'S T. THOMAS FORTUNE?

By Rick Geffken

"I believe in the divine right of man, not of caste or class."
—*T. Thomas Fortune, the* New York Freeman, *May 1, 1886*

The crusading T. Thomas Fortune was adamant about using the term "Afro-American," because, he said, the descendants of slaves are "African in origin and American in birth." Born enslaved in 1856 in Florida, Fortune rose above that circumstance to such prominence that he became an associate of other twentieth-century black leaders like Booker T. Washington and Marcus Garvey.

In 1901, he and his wife, Carrie, moved to Red Bank, which was close to the trains he took to New York City. He bought an 1870s Second Empire–style home on Beech Street with a mansard roof and called it "Maple Hall." T. Thomas Fortune left Red Bank for good around 1915, after he and his wife separated. The house eventually became the private home and bakery of the Vaccarelli family. Maple Hall was listed in the National Register of Historic Places in 1976 and the New Jersey Register of Historic Places in 1979, but Fortune's fate was that of a forgotten man for almost a century.

Besides his *New York Freeman* newspaper, Fortune also published the *New York Age*, which he envisioned as "the Afro-American Journal of News and Opinion." Well-known journalists Victoria Earle Matthews and Ida B. Wells reported for his paper. Fortune also led the Afro-American Press Association, raising the standards of black professional journalism throughout the country.

T. Thomas Fortune, born enslaved in Florida, moved to Red Bank in 1901, when he was a crusading journalist. *New York Public Library.*

Fortune wrote his first book, *Black and White: Land, Labor, and Politics in the South*, in 1884, when he was twenty-eight years old and had lived for twenty years a free man of color. He published *Dreams of Life: Miscellaneous Poems* in 1905.

According to Lynn Humphreys of the T. Thomas Fortune Foundation, "Fortune passed away from heart disease on June 2, 1928, at the age of seventy-one in Philadelphia, Pennsylvania. He was buried in an unmarked grave in Eden Cemetery, Collingdale, Pennsylvania, never regaining the influence he held during the first decade of the twentieth century as a leader in the movement for African American rights."

For more details about the man and his life, visit: http://www. tthomasfortuneculturalcenter.org/.

—Previously unpublished

48

TINTON FALLS CRAWFORD HOUSE

By Rick Geffken

The recently restored Crawford House in Tinton Falls will be the centerpiece for interpreting the beginnings of Monmouth County. Tinton Falls—the huge Morris family manor estate and the actual scenic waterway it was built around—are inseparable from the cultural richness of the historic Two Rivers area. After almost ten years of scraping, sanding, painting and the removal of modern additions, Stacey Slowinski and the Friends of the Crawford House debuted the reconstituted nineteenth century home as a museum during the annual Weekend in Old Monmouth, which was held on May 6 and 7, 2017.

Slowinski, president of the Friends of the Crawford House, is thrilled that the home to four generations of the Crawford family has been added to the list of the many sites open to visitors during the annual springtime celebration of Monmouth County history. The Friends of the Crawford House just completed renovating the borough-owned building, which sits on five acres fronting Tinton Avenue. The group hopes "to broaden the scope of the Crawford House's impact—to make it alive and vibrant," Slowinski says.

Besides being a stop on the spring event in 2017, the Crawford House's ambitious schedule for the future will likely feature music and poetry nights, cooking demonstrations and local history talks and lectures. The Friends of the Crawford House also expect to host repeat "Tomato Fests" based on the positive responses to their gardening and recipe-sharing demonstrations. Reprises of "Colonial Days" will surely attract audiences, too. The Friends

The Crawford House in Tinton Falls is on the site of the seventeenth-century Tintern Manor Iron Works. *Andres Palomino, Friends of the Crawford House.*

of the Crawford House are busy enlisting new members and finalizing details for these and other future events.

New discoveries about the Crawford House are starting to emerge. "Just the other day, I came upstairs and found a survey of the property which we didn't know we had. We think a lot of exciting things will show up once we're officially opened to the public," said Slowinski.

Ruth and Allen Crawford were the last of the family to live at the house, which is located just across the road from the falls and borders Pine Brook. "Ruth died in 1986." says Slowinski. "Just recently, a Crawford in-law donated Ruth's piano to us. We put it back in the dining room where it stood for many years. When Allen Crawford was the Tinton Falls tax collector in the 1920s, people stopping by to pay their taxes at the little office on the front porch of the house and would often spend some time playing musical instruments with Ruth at the piano."

For decades, the Crawfords operated a slaughterhouse and butcher shop on their property; these were started around 1860 by Allen's grandfather John H. Crawford in what was then Shrewsbury. Long before, the property was where Lewis Morris operated his Tintern Manor Iron Works. Morris bought thousands of acres of property in East Jersey in 1679. He brought his Barbados slaves with him to run the iron and gristmills powered by the falls of Shrewsbury. The Morris family originated in Monmouthshire in Wales, and it is believed that Lewis commemorated his birthplace by naming our county for it. Tintern Abbey in Wales inspired the name of his estate.

Several years ago, a survey team looked around the Crawford property for the remains of a slave cemetery depicted on early Morris maps. Though some intriguing anomalies were recorded by ground-penetrating radar, Dr. Richard Veit of Monmouth University was hesitant to identify any as the graves of slaves. Slowinski noted that "Dr. Veit was not surprised by the many 'disturbances' found in the survey. We think a barn may have been built over the graveyard at some point in the long history of the land."

The Friends of the Crawford House is a nonprofit group formed to act as steward and advocate for the Crawford House, its history and its property. For more information about volunteering or upcoming events, contact Stacey Slowinski at sslowinski@verizon.net.

—From the *Two River Times*, April 20, 2017

49

HISTORY WINDS THROUGH RUMSON'S ROADS

by Rick Geffken

From the Rumson County Club to Jumping Point, Rumson Road's mix of luxurious homes, lush landscapes and river views are unparalleled. This gently curving thoroughfare was central to the development of Rumson from the beginning. It also played a major role in the growth of Monmouth County.

The millennia-old Lenape Great Trail footpath was renamed the "Burlington Trail" by early white settlers. At its eastern end, which leads to the Shrewsbury River and the Atlantic Ocean, the trail traversed the long neck of land called Navarumsunk. The 1665 deed from the Navesink band of Lenapes to English settlers from Gravesend (Brooklyn) called the two rivers defining Navarumsunk the Shushopponoring (Navesink) and the Arummanend (Shrewsbury). Popomora, an Indian sachem who signed the deed with his X, is memorialized on Rumson's Popomora Drive. John Hance had five hundred acres, river to river, but it took two more centuries for Rumson to develop into a real town.

Ore carts from Lewis Morris's Tinton Falls Ironworks, sometimes called the Tintern Manor Iron Works, traveled along the Rumson Neck road as early as 1680. English and Dutch settlers loaded their wagons with produce and used the same road to Passage Point (Black Point), so-called because sailing ships "passed" through inlets on their way to the New York with Monmouth County crops. This county's agricultural success seemed to be assured.

In the mid-nineteenth century, Martinus Bergen opened a tomato-canning factory close to the Navesink. Steamboats docked at Washington Street, offloading visitors who stayed at Thomas Hunt's Port Washington Pavilion Hotel. The little village of Port Washington was renamed Oceanic in 1845, and thereafter, Hunt subdivided his vast acreage into residential lots. Another spurt of building occurred round the time Michael Rainey Jr. bought a lot in 1884 and put up the twenty-two-room Lafayette Hotel (which later became home to the Russell & Bette's restaurant).

The 1870 Jumping Point Drawbridge at the eastern end of Rumson Road connected the verdant peninsula to the oceanfront barrier-beach towns. Jumping Point was where Patriot Joshua Huddy escaped from the British in 1780 by jumping into the Shrewsbury River.

As Rumson historian Roberta H. Van Anda notes in *Legendary Locals of Rumson*, "Giants of finance, industry, politics, commerce, science, and the arts arrived in the late 1800s by train or steamboat and summered in fashionable Long Branch and Seabright." When the inlets finally sanded over, steamboats from Rumson navigated the Shrewsbury River before rounding Sandy Hook on their way to New York City.

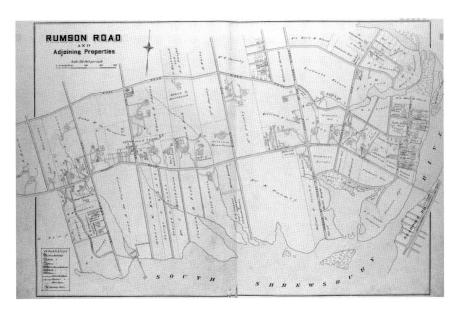

Wolverton's *Atlas of Monmouth County* showed Rumson and Ridge Roads running east–west through the borough in 1889. *New York Public Library.*

Successful businessmen from such diverse industries as textile manufacturing (Matthew Borden), brewing (John Gillig and Christian Feigenspan) and politics (Cornelius Bliss) made Rumson their summer or country home. Historian Randall Gabrielan notes that "Thomas N. McCarter was the first major city figure to make Rumson his year-round home."

In his latest documentary, *Rumson Hill*, filmmaker Chris Brenner tells the story of "one wealthy attorney and industrialist [who] decided to make Rumson his permanent home and created one of the most iconic estates in New Jersey history." That man was Thomas Nesbitt McCarter. His 421-acre estate (including what is still known as McCarter Pond decades after his death) spanned the two-river peninsula from Rumson Road to the Navesink River.

McCarter was the attorney general of New Jersey and the first president of the Public Service Electric & Gas utility conglomerate. He bought the Kemp estate in Rumson in 1905 for the equivalent of $3.8 million in today's dollars. Three years later, he sold 213 acres of the western portion to the Rumson Country Club.

An award-winning filmmaker, Brenner grew up in Rumson, playing high school football for the Bulldogs. *Rumson Hill* showcases McCarter's sprawling grounds, with the sumptuous three-floor mansion built at the peninsula's highest elevation. With its copper-clad roof, an elevator and deep-hewed hardwoods interior, the McCarter home afforded spectacular views in all directions, with a huge formal garden, horse stables and barns and a swimming pool, as well as staff and maintenance outbuildings.

McCarter built an arched and ivy-covered bridge over Ridge Road to avoid traffic congestion at the intersection with the entry road to his home. McCarter's overpass outlived its creator, who died in 1953. The bridge was seen as the unofficial border between Fair Haven and Rumson. The deteriorating structure became a graffiti-laden traffic hazard before it was finally demolished in 1988.

Rumson Town Hall's George H. Moss Jr. Room, named for the late Rumson historian and author, contains many remarkable maps, historical photos and documents. The Borough of Rumson, formally established in 1907, now contains forty miles of roads, including 133 streets and 5 county roads within its five square miles. But the Lenape footpath that morphed into a colonial wagon road was the beginning of it all.

—From the *Two River Times*, March 8–15, 2018

50

How the Rumson–Fair Haven Bulldogs Got That Name

By Rick Geffken

O nce a bulldog, always a bulldog," says Rumson–Fair Haven Regional High School principal Dr. Tracy Handerhan. Famous for its stamina, strength and persistence, the tenacious canine does seem an especially appropriate mascot for the school's sports teams. The mush-faced dogs come in colors dubbed red brindle, black brindle, pure white, grey or black. So, why are the Rumson Bulldogs purple and white?

According to historian and longtime board of education member Roberta Van Anda, the story of the nickname involves a fierce young boxer from Elizabeth, New Jersey, named Mickey Walker. During a boxing career that spanned from 1919 to 1935, Walker won the world welterweight and middleweight boxing titles. Early in his career, it turns out that he trained in Rumson.

Two River Times contributor Muriel Smith treasures a framed newspaper article written by her father, Vincent dePaul Slavin, a professional reporter. Slavin visited Walker's Rumson training camp in June 1921. Writing for a small Elizabeth weekly, Slavin watched the rising boxing phenom prepare for his first big fight with welterweight champion Jack Britton. "Mickey has been training hard for the past three weeks for the 'fight of his life' at his camp in Rumson, three miles from Red Bank," wrote Slavin.

"Every morning at seven sharp found Walker tumbling out of the hay down stairs for his cup of tea and a few pieces of toast," he continued. "At eight o'clock he started on the road and with his many supporters,

Mickey Walker was an internationally known boxer who trained in Rumson, New Jersey. *Fotograms, N.Y.*

second, sparring partners and mascots, covered three miles through the hills of Monmouth County." Those "mascots" were local schoolboys in awe of their boxing hero. (Mickey Walker not only found running the local hills of Rumson, Ridge and River Roads ideal for conditioning, he also found nearby Sea Bright just as ideal for running a sideline bootleg booze business some years later, during the Depression.)

In January 1923, Walker married Maude Kelly, a Brooklyn woman he met while she summered at her mother's Lafayette Street house in Rumson. Walker bought his mother-in-law's house and remodeled it, and the young couple moved in with her. In a biography of the fighter, he quipped "I paid her nine thousand dollars, and she came with the house."

A sports editor of the *New York Evening Mail* named Francis Albertanti came up with the sobriquet that Walker himself called "one of the greatest ever hung on anybody in the ring." The writer christened Walker the "Toy Bulldog." By the end of the 1920s, news reports all over the country were referring to the feisty fighter as the "Rumson Bulldog."

Rumson High School played its very first football game (a 12–6 victory over Leonardo) in October 1934. Newspaper reports called them "the blue and white" but did not mention a nickname. Searching through the school's *Tower* yearbooks, high school librarian Linda Murray discovered that 1940 was the first year the football team was called the "Rumson Bulldogs." (Incidentally, Murray says, "We're missing only one yearbook from our eighty-three-year collection. If anyone can donate a 1939 yearbook, I'd be very grateful.") Apparently, around the time the new high school was built on Ridge Road, many locals recalled Walker's training runs—his nickname was the perfect fit.

Bertram Borden, the owner of a successful printing and textile businesses, was then the president of the Rumson Board of Education. The new high school, dedicated in 1936, was a Works Progress Administration (WPA) Depression-era project. Borden and his wife, Mary, held a Rumson Garden Club Flower Show at their estate every year.

Van Anda recalled two stories about the inspiration for the school colors. "The story I had was from men who were on the first athletic teams. The boys lived in the Lafayette Street area near where Mickey Walker lived, and he let them run with him when he trained. His colors on his boxing trunks and robe were purple and white. He was their hero, and they adopted the colors in his honor."

She continued, "Bertram Borden was on the school board and had a great deal to do with getting the old Rumson High School approved by the voters and constructed. The football field behind the school was later named in his honor. His wife, Mary Owen Borden, loved the purple-and-white Beaconsfield pansy, and he wore one in his lapel in her memory. It would make sense that the [school-colors] choice of the students conformed with Bertram Borden's selection. So, both stories have credence. Mark Hughes wrote a history of the Borden Scholarship, and he used the Bertram Borden story. The early athletes told me the Mickey Walker story. The stories probably blended at the board of education."

And that's how a rough prizefighter, and, just maybe, a delicate flower—surely one of the most unlikely combinations imaginable—inspired this proud community's high school nickname and colors.

—From the *Two River Times*, March 8–15, 2018

51

THE RUMSON BULLDOG CONNECTION

By Muriel J. Smith

Rick Geffken's terrific story in the *Two River Times* about boxer Mickey Walker and how the Rumson–Fair Haven teams got their bulldog nickname prompted me to share a personal story that involves not only the boxer, but also my dad, and explains why I am a writer. It's something I can't help—I inherited the passion.

Rick's research—and it's always extensive—included reviewing an article written by my father, Vincent dePaul Slavin (always Vincent dePaul, never Vince or Vincent DePaul, to be sure that St. Vincent dePaul was always honored), who was a young reporter when Walker was training in Rumson.

It was 1921, and my father was twenty-four at the time and writing for the *Index and Elizabeth Review*, billed as "the only Sunday newspaper in Union County." His byline on the story identifies him as a special correspondent to the paper, which means he was probably writing for several different papers at the time (another gene I inherited). He was raised in Philadelphia, and somehow, the family found their way to Elizabeth, New Jersey—probably because his father got a job with the Esso refinery. He had met my mother, Gladys Van Den Bergh, but it would be another four years before the couple married and settled in Union.

Mickey Walker was about twenty-one at the time; he was born in Elizabeth and lived in Newark and was scheduled to wage "the fight of his life" against Jack Britton, another Irishman, who held the welterweight title. My father thought the story was important and "local" enough to wrangle his way into hanging around Walker for an entire day while the

Vincent dePaul Slavin, inveterate news reporter, religious leader and family man, died too young in 1945. *Slavin family.*

boxer trained in and around his home on Lafayette Street in Rumson. The story, written in the flowing, adjective-filled prose of the day, captured some of the beauty of the area, as well as the training techniques of Walker and his training team.

My father hadn't spent much time in Monmouth County; it would be another ten years (and a few more children) before he brought his family to enjoy the beach at Sandlass Beach Club, located across the river from

Highlands. He described Walker's Rumson training camp as being "three miles" from the more famous town of Red Bank.

You could tell Vince Slavin loved the area. Despite the story being about the soon-to-be welterweight champion, my father, the sports reporter, took space to write: "Two blocks from the shore of the Shrewsbury River, in the rear of a bungalow well shaded with huge maple trees, there stands a little house, one story high, and containing but one room. In this room, Mickey went through a good bit of his hard work."

Later in the article, he writes: "Every morning at seven sharp found Mickey tumbling out of the hay down stairs for his cup of tea and a few pieces of toast. At eight o'clock he started on the road, and with his many supporters, second, sparring partners and mascots, covered three miles through the hills of Monmouth County."

The story goes on to talk about the run, the rubdowns after, the finishing order of the rest of the team and a nap for the champ, then launches back into the charm of Monmouth County and its people. This group of people, including my dad, Walker's chauffeur and a few others, sat down for "a good old-fashioned country meal," where "the good old country mother at whose home the challenger boarded, spread on the table fried potatoes, egg salad (that couldn't be beat) frankfurters, rolls and tea."

After lunch, the story continues, "all hands bounced into Bulger's [Walker's manager, Jack Bulger] auto and rode two blocks to the water front where Joe Higgins and Gillie had a chance to show their fancy diving wares.…Mickey sat on the rear of the pier with a fair damsel who showed him how to knit." The reporter added, "up until two weeks ago, Walker battled with the waves daily, but for the last few days Bulger wouldn't permit his charge to take to the inviting waves of the Shrewsbury."

Nor could Walker enjoy the festivities at Borden's skating rink with the rest of his crew. While they donned skates to enjoy the rink, Walker wasn't permitted (by his manager) to skate, the story said, for fear he might fall and injure himself.

Walker went on to a disputed decision in that bout but came back the next year to claim the title and again to take the middleweight title from Tiger Flowers. Later yet, he went eight rounds as a heavyweight against Max Schmeling. Walker retired in 1935, opened a pub in Elizabeth and took up art, painting and exhibiting both still lifes and scenery. Sadly, in 1974, Freehold police found him lying alongside the road and took him for a homeless alcoholic. Actually, he was suffering from Parkinson's disease, atherosclerosis and anemia and spent the next few years in a variety of care centers and hospitals. He died on April 28, 1981, at Freehold Area Hospital.

My dad went on to be the police reporter for the *Newark Evening News*, covering everything from the *Hindenburg* explosion at Lakewood to Dutch Schulz's murder on the street in Newark, as well as hospital ships returning with injured GIs during World War II. He died suddenly in 1945 nine days before Christmas. But he left me, his youngest daughter, with a gift for which I'll always be grateful.

—From the *Atlantic Highlands Journal*, March 19, 2018

LENAPE LEGACY ON THE NAVESINK

By Rick Geffken

Hundreds of years before the Oyster Point Hotel and Marina opened on the banks of the Navesink River in 1986, a band of Lenape feasted on those succulent shellfish and left behind a huge thirty-foot-wide by fifteen-foot-high midden of oyster shells. These piles of shells were found all along the Bayshore and helped archaeologists determine much about how our Native American predecessors lived on our Two River estuaries, according to Claire Thomas Garland.

Garland, the director of the Sand Hill Indian Historical Association, gave an informative talk, "500 Years on the Navesink," at the Eisner Memorial Red Bank Public Library on Saturday, August 11, 2018. She brought along her sizable collection of artifacts from her Native American ancestry—leather shirts and pants, a feathered fan, gourd rattles and pictures of her Revey family ancestors, whom she dates to 1780. Their heritage lingers in a section of Tinton Falls still called Reveytown, which is located along and around Shafto Road in that borough. It was named for Thomas Revey during the nineteenth century.

Sand Hill in Neptune was the location of one of her ancestor's homes. The area near today's West Bangs Avenue is occasionally used today for family reunions.

"History didn't begin here with Columbus in 1492," Garland told the attentive audience of adults and children. "European fishing boats were trading with natives along the coast down through Massachusetts in the thirteenth century." Even farther south, Indians, as they were wrongly described by Columbus and other explorers, were aware of these strange-looking men sailing along their coastal waters.

Garland's ancestry is a mix of native Lenape, Cherokee (who had moved from Georgia to New Jersey) and colonial Dutch. The Revey family included many artisans who created traditional Native American clothing and other useful articles to help support themselves. Lenape influence on European culture after first contact was substantial in surprising ways. "When the Europeans started arriving in the New World, they dressed in shorty-shorts and high stockings," noted Garland. "They quickly learned to wear leather pants, like the Indians, to prevent briars from cutting their legs."

Place names—or "Indian talk," as Garland called it—that we take for granted now were originally Lenape designations: Wanamassa, Mantoloking, Matawan, Manasquan, Wickatunk and, yes, even Navesink and Rumson. The last two derived from variations of the name of the Navesinck band of Lenape and the peninsula they referred to as Narumsunk.

Garland pointed out that the late Paul Boyd, of Atlantic Highlands, who wrote *From Lenape Camps to Bayside Town*, believed that the shell middens he

Sand Hill Indian chief Ryers Crummal (*center*) is pictured—along with tribe-member relatives who shared Lenape and Cherokee heritage—in Neptune in 1949. *Claire T. Garland.*

found every eight miles along the shoreline indicated Indian villages about a day's walk from each other. Until Europeans appeared, Native Americans believed in communal rights to property, with everyone sharing in the land's riches. When the Indians "signed" deeds (mostly by making a mark like an "X"), they thought of them like leases. The European concept of hard rights to property essentially let the Europeans steal land. The New Jersey State Archives has preserved over eight hundred of these deeds.

An interesting aspect of Garland's talk was her assertion that during the last Ice Age, the water captured as ice at the North Pole reduced the Atlantic Ocean to the extent that our coastline was eighty miles out from where it is today. She claimed that Native Americans built villages and houses on this extended shelf, though few remains of them have ever been found.

Other revelations from Garland included that the Turtle Clan of the Lenape occupied most of the middle section of New Jersey in our area. "Lenape people hunted seals, whales, porpoises. They supplemented their diets with fruit like apples, quince and beach plums. Europeans were in awe of the abundance in the local estuaries here. They sent letters back home encouraging more settlers to come to the New World, where they would find 'a whole cellar of food.'"

Garland also mentioned, seemingly without rancor, that "The County of Monmouth took 105 acres of my family's property at Reveytown to construct the Reclamation Center along Shafto Road." One might wonder if the pungent odor in the area is something of a Lenape revenge.

For more about Garland's Revey and Sand Hill Indian ancestry, visit sandhillindianhistory.org.

—From the *Two River Times*, August 23, 2018

BIBLIOGRAPHY

Adelberg, Michael S. *The American Revolution in Monmouth County*. Charleston, SC: The History Press, 2010.

———. *Roster of the People of Revolutionary Monmouth County (NJ)*. Baltimore, MD: Genealogical Publishing Company, 2003.

Ansted, A. *A Dictionary of Sea Terms*. Glasgow, Scotland: Brown, Son & Ferguson, Ltd., 1972.

Barber, John W. *Historical Collections of New Jersey*. New York: S. Tuttle, 1846.

Beekman, George C. *Early Dutch Settlers of Monmouth County New Jersey*. Freehold, NJ: Moreau Bros., 1901.

Beers, Comstock and Cline. *Atlas of Monmouth County, New Jersey*. New York: Beers, Comstock and Cline, 1873.

Boyd, Paul D. *Atlantic Highlands: From Lenape Camps to Bayside Town*. Charleston SC: Arcadia Publishing, 2004.

Brown, James S. *Allaire's Lost Empire*. Freehold, NJ: The Transcript Printing House, 1958.

Burke, Dorothy. *History of Farmingdale*. Farmingdale, NJ: Farmingdale Public School, 1965.

Burr, Nelson R. *The Anglican Church in New Jersey*. Philadelphia, PA: The Church Historical Society, 1954.

Christ Church. *Christ Church Vestry Minutes*. Shrewsbury, NJ: Christ Church, 1768–1900.

Colts Neck Historical Committee. *History of Colts Neck*. Colts Neck, NJ: Colts Neck Historical Committee, 1964.

Cronk, Judith B. *Intestates and Others from the Orphans Court Books of Monmouth County, 1785–1906*. Baltimore, MD: Clearfield Company, 2002.

Donahay, Alma. *History of Howell*. Howell, NJ: Howell Historical Society, 1982.

Ellis, Franklin. *History of Monmouth County, New Jersey*. Philadelphia, PA: R.T. Peck & Co., 1885.

Gabrielan, Randall. *The American Century Series: Tinton Falls in the Twentieth Century*. Charleston, SC: Arcadia Publishing, 1999.

———. *Middletown Township, Volume III*. Charleston, SC: Arcadia Publishing, 1997.

———. *Monmouth County, New Jersey*. Charleston, SC: Arcadia Publishing, 1998.

Geffken, Rick, and Don Burden. *The Story of Shrewsbury, Revisited 1965–2015*. Shrewsbury, NJ: Shrewsbury Historical Society, 2015.

Geffken, Rick, and George Severini. *Lost Amusement Parks of the North Jersey Shore*. Charleston, SC: Arcadia Publishing, 2017.

Gibson, George and Florence. *Marriages of Monmouth County, 1795–1843*. Baltimore, MD: Clearfield Co., 1992.

Gillingham, Evan S., Jr., ed. *The Story of Eatontown*. Eatontown, NJ: Eatontown Tricentennial Committee, 1970.

Gordon, Thomas F. *A Gazetteer of the State of New Jersey*. Trenton, NJ: Daniel Fenton, 1834.

Grabas, Joseph A. *Owning New Jersey, Historic Tales of War, Property Disputes & the Pursuit of Happiness*. Charleston, SC: The History Press, 2014.

Hodges, Graham Russell. *Slavery and Freedom in the Rural North: African Americans in Monmouth County, New Jersey, 1665–1865*. Lanham, MD: Madison House Publishers, 1997.

Hornor, William S. *This Old Monmouth of Ours*. Freehold, NJ: Moreau Brothers, 1932.

Hunton, Gail, and James C. McCabe. *Monmouth County Historic Sites Summary Report, 1980–1984*. Trenton, NJ: Office of New Jersey Heritage, 1984.

Hutchinson, Richard S. *Monmouth County Deeds, Books A, B, C, and D*. Westminster, MD: Heritage Books, 2006.

Jerseyana Club of Shrewsbury School. *Shrewsbury Century Homes, Part 1*. Shrewsbury, NJ: Shrewsbury Boro School, 1964.

Kiernan, Mary Ann. *The Monmouth Patent, Part I and Part II*. Red Bank, NJ: The Greater Red Bank Voice, 1986 and 1988.

Kobbé, Gustav. *The New Jersey Coast and Pines*. New York: Gustav Kobbé Company, 1891.

Kraybill, Richard L. *The Story of Shrewsbury, 1664–1964*. Red Bank, NJ: The Commercial Press, 1964.

Leeds, Benjamin Franklin. *Thomas Leeds, an Englishman, Settled at Shrewsbury, NJ, Probably in 1677*. Philadelphia: 1886.

Leonard, Thomas H. *From Indian Trail to Electric Rail*. Atlantic Highlands, NJ: *Atlantic Highlands Journal*, 1923.

Lewis Historical Publications. *History of Monmouth County, New Jersey, 1664–1920*. New York and Chicago: Lewis Historical Publishing, 1922.

Little, Donald Campbell. *Descendants of Col. John Little, Esq., of Shrewsbury Township, Monmouth County, New Jersey*. Edwardsville, KS: Donald C. Little, 1951.

Martin, George Castor. *The Shark River District, Monmouth County, NJ and Genealogies of Chambers, Corlies, Drummond, Morris, Potter, Shafto, Webley, and White*. Asbury Park, NJ: Martin & Allardyce, 1914.

McConville, Brendan. *These Daring Disturbers of the Public Peace*. Philadelphia: University of Pennsylvania, 1999.

Methot, June. *Up and Down the River*. Navesink, NJ: Whip Publishers, 1980.

Miles, Anne Pette. *Monmouth Families, Vol. I*. King William, VA: Anne Pette Miles, 1980.

Monmouth County Archives. "Revolution Papers, Inquisitions & Confiscations, 1778–1801." Unpublished.

———. "Slave Births, 1804–1848." Unpublished.

———. "Slave Manumissions, 1787–1844." Unpublished.

Monmouth County Historical Association Collections. "Knott Family Genealogy in the Collections of Barbara Carver Smith." Unpublished.

———. "Tinton Falls Iron Works Records 1668–1761." Unpublished.

Moss, George, Jr. *Monmouth, Our Indian Heritage*. Freehold, NJ: Monmouth County Historical Commission, 1974.

National Archives and Records Administration. "Earle Naval Weapons Station Records."

Nelson, William. *The New Jersey Coast in Three Centuries*. New York and Chicago: Lewis Historical Publishing, 1902.

Nelson, William, ed. *Documents Relating to the Colonial History of the State of New Jersey*. Newark, NJ: *Newark Daily Journal*, 1880–1886.

———. *Extracts from American Newspapers, Relating to New Jersey, 1704–1775*. Paterson, NJ: The Call Printing and Publishing Company, 1904.

New Jersey Office of Historic Preservation. *Farmingdale District, Historic Sites Inventory*. Trenton, NJ: Office of Historic Preservation, 1982.

New-York Historical Society. *Collections of the New-York Historical Society for the Year 1895.* New York: New-York Historical Society, 1896.

Office of Monmouth County Clerk. *Town by Town, Impressions of Monmouth County.* Freehold, NJ: Monmouth County Clerk, 2002.

Parris, Frederic J. *The Case of Reverend Samuel Cooke: Loyalist.* Freehold, NJ: Monmouth County Historical Society, 1975.

Phillips, Helen C. *Red Bank on the Navesink.* Red Bank, NJ: Caesarea Press, 1977.

Raser, Edward J. *New Jersey Graveyard & Gravestone Inscriptions Locators: Monmouth County.* New Brunswick, NJ: Genealogical Society of New Jersey, 2002.

Rose, T.F., H.C. Woolman and T.T. Price. *Historical and Biographical Atlas of the New Jersey Coast.* Philadelphia, PA: Woolman & Rose, 1878.

Rumson Historical Committee. *History of Rumson, 1665–1944.* Asbury Park, NJ: Schuyler Press, 1944.

Salter, Edwin. *Old Times in Old Monmouth.* Freehold, NJ: *Monmouth Democrat*, 1874.

Schirber, Eric R. "The King's Friends in Monmouth County." *New Jersey Historical Commission* (Trenton) *Newsletter*, 1975.

Shrewsbury (NJ) Historical Society. "Collections." Shrewsbury, NJ: Unpublished.

Smith, Muriel J. *I Know How to Grieve, I Want to Learn How to Laugh.* Atlantic Highlands, NJ: Gateway Press, 2006.

———. *The Reporter and the Draft: The World War II Story of a Journalist Turned Renegade Draft Board Chairman.* Akron, OH: 48Hr Books, 2007.

———. *Twenty-Five Years of Excellence: The New Jersey Alliance for Action, Inc.* Edison, NJ: New Jersey Alliance for Action, 1999.

Steen, James. *History of Christ Church, Shrewsbury, New Jersey, 1702–1903.* New Jersey: 1903.

———. *New Aberdeen, or, The Scotch Settlement of Monmouth County, New Jersey.* Matawan, NJ: Journal Steam Print, 1899.

Stillwell, John Edwin. *First Families of Old Monmouth.* New York: 1882.

Van Anda, Roberta H. *Legendary Locals of Rumson.* Charleston, SC: Arcadia Publishing, 2015.

Veit, Richard, and Maxine N. Lurie, eds. *New Jersey, A History of the Garden State.* New Brunswick, NJ: Rutgers University Press, 2012.

Whitehead, William A., ed. *The Papers of Lewis Morris, Governor of the Province of New Jersey, from 1738–1746.* New York: George P. Putnam, 1852.

Wilson, Harold F. *The Story of the Jersey Shore.* Princeton, NJ: Van Nostrand, 1964.

Wolverton, Chester. *Atlas of Monmouth County, New Jersey*. New York: Chester Wolverton, 1889.

Wright, Giles. *Afro-Americans in New Jersey, A Short History*. Trenton: New Jersey Historical Commission, 1988.

INDEX

M

R

S

About the Authors

Rick Geffken and Muriel J. Smith. *Scott D. Longfield.*

Rick Geffken's earliest and happiest memories are from the years he summered at the Jersey Shore. He's lived or worked in Middletown, Highlands, Eatontown, Rumson, Holmdel, Long Branch, Spring Lake and Brielle. After retiring from a career in the computer industry, he moved to Farmingdale and began historical research, which led to the publication of his first book (with Don Burden), *The Story of Shrewsbury Revisited, 1965–2015*. Together, he and George Severini wrote *Lost Amusement Parks of the North Jersey Shore* (Arcadia Publishing).

A popular speaker at many New Jersey historical societies, Rick has published numerous historical articles for the *Two River Times*; the *Howell Times*; *Edge* magazine; several Patch blogs; the *Crown* newsletter of Christ Episcopal Church, Shrewsbury; and the *Monmouth Connection* newsletter, a publication of the Monmouth County Genealogy Society (he was also the publisher of the *Monmouth Connection*).

Rick is a decorated Vietnam veteran; he served as a U.S. Army Intelligence Officer in 1969–70 during that conflict. He is a trustee of the Shrewsbury Historical Society, a past president and a trustee of the Jersey Coast Heritage Museum at Sandlass House and a member of the Monmouth County Historical Association.

Rick is working on another book about the historians of Monmouth County, past and present, and has at least three others in mind, plus maybe a play, a novel and a few video projects.

Rick is actively researching, writing and lecturing about the integral part enslaved Africans and their descendants have played in New Jersey. He is helping to infuse African American history studies into Monmouth County schools, notably the Shrewsbury Boro School, as per New Jersey's Amistad Commission recommendations.

Muriel J. Smith is a born writer, inheriting the passion from her newspaper journalist father and sharing it with her journalist brother, Vincent dePaul Jr. A native of Union, she fell in love with her husband, James E. Smith Jr., and Highlands at the same time and found a new passion in writing about the history of the county where she has lived for more than six decades

A graduate of Mount St. Mary's in North Plainfield, Muriel wrote for several weekly and daily newspapers before becoming editor of the *Courier* in Middletown and editor for Forbes NJ Newspapers. She has authored three books: *The NJ Alliance for Action: 25 Years of Progress*; *The Reporter and the Draft*, the story of her father's role as draft board chairman in World War II; and *I Know How to Grieve, I Want to Learn How to Laugh*, a self-help book she wrote after her husband's death in 2006.

Muriel is a member of the Monmouth County Historical Commission and a former member of the Freehold Borough Historic Preservation Commission, as well as several municipal historic societies. An award-winning journalist in investigative, political and news reporting, she also served on the Highlands Board of Education and was secretary of the Atlantic Highlands–Highlands Regional Sewerage Authority. She is a public relations writer for the Monmouth County Library Commission, mediator for New Jersey Civil Court, patient advocate for the New Jersey Department of the Elderly and a CCD instructor at both St. Rose of Lima Parish in Freehold and Our Lady of Perpetual Help–St. Agnes Parish in Atlantic Highlands.

In February 2019, working with Congressman Chris Smith, she was successful in securing respect for Congressional Medal of Honor recipient

James Fallon, a Civil War hero from Freehold, by having his Medal of Honor removed from the Pennsylvania college where it was being used to represent a similar honor for an alumnus of the college and presented to a Fallon family member, fellow Monmouth County Historical Commissioner Glenn Cashion. It will ultimately be on display at the Monmouth County Historical Association. Working with Friends of the Twin Lights director Mark Stewart, she was also responsible for having Medal of Honor recipient Robert Blume, who received the Medal of Honor for heroism in the Spanish-American War, honored with a display at the Twin Lights in Highlands, where he became a lighthouse keeper after his service in the U.S. Navy.

Visit us at
www.historypress.com
....